THE WAY OF THE
SACRED
TREE

EDNA
HONG

AUGSBURG Publishing House • Minneapolis

THE WAY OF THE SACRED TREE

Copyright © 1983 Augsburg Publishing House

Library of Congress Catalog Card No. 82-072643

International Standard Book No. 0-8066-1949-X

Scripture quotations unless otherwise noted are from the Revised Standard Version of the Bible, copyright 1946, 1952, and 1971 by the Division of Christian Education of the National Council of Churches.

Manufactured in the United States of America

THE WAY OF THE
SACRED
TREE

To the loving memory of
"Aunt Jane"
and all the Dakota girls
who out of love of Jane Williamson
were named Jane

The eyes of the person who is conscious of himself as a single individual are formed to see everything contrary; his mentality becomes intimate with eternity's truth—that everything in life shows up as opposite.

—Søren Kierkegaard

Contents

One
One *Wakan* Night/ 11
Two
The Corn Was Plump with Milk/ 17
Three
The New Moon Has Two Horns/ 22
Four
The Fork in the Trail/ 27
Five
Every New Day Is *Wakan*/ 32
Six
Of Happy Things and Curious Things and an Evil Thing/ 38
Seven
Ask the Deepest Place in Your Heart/ 45
Eight
A New Name/ 51
Nine
They Carry But Little/ 57
Ten
Kaposia/ 65
Eleven
Whys That Buzz Like Flies/ 72
Twelve
Great Mystery, Is That All?/ 80

Thirteen
How Does One Become a Warrior Without a War?/ 88
Fourteen
Fuel for the Conflagration/ 97
Fifteen
On the Reservation/ 105
Sixteen
John Has Come!/ 113
Seventeen
Let Them Eat Grass!/ 126
Eighteen
What I Have Done, I Have Done/ 135
Nineteen
I Killed! I Killed!/ 143
Twenty
So This Is What It Is to Be a Christian!/ 150
Twenty-One
So This, Then, Was the Meaning!/ 157
Twenty-Two
To See That, They Need the Crossed Eyes of a *Heyoka*/ 166
Twenty-Three
This Is Indeed a New Thing/ 176
Twenty-Four
The Sign of Contradiction/ 182
Epilog/ 190
Glossary/ 199
Acknowledgments/ 202

1

One *Wakan* Night

He was born on that never-to-be-forgotten night in the Moon When the Deer Rut when the sky rained stars and the noon of night became as bright as the noon of day. While his father and uncle-fathers and mother-uncles stood watch with the other warriors and counselors on the ridge above the village on the Lac qui Parle, the Lake That Speaks, Hapanna knelt in her grandmother's *tipi* and gave him birth. While his aunt-mothers and father-aunts and the other women of the village clustered under the shooting stars on that night of mystery and made fear-and-trembling cries, Uncida, his grandmother, and Hapanna, his mother, washed him with warm water in which Uncida had steeped a sweet-smelling grass. She dusted his navel with the powder of a puffball, laid him on a clean new deerskin, and tucked soft cattail-down under and around his buttocks.

Wrapping him close, Hapanna picked him up, her secondborn child, her firstborn son, and stepped from her mother's *tipi* out under the great sky-*tipi* that was as bright at midnight as at midday. She pulled back the flap of deerskin from her son's face so that he, too, could look up at the sky. Uncida stood beside her, and it was as if the three of them were looking in humble amazement as one. Holding the small bundle up to the mystery in the sky, Hapanna sang a whispering song, a prayer song. Like the song of the brown thrasher, her song repeated each joy-line:

11

My son! My son!
Born in mystery!
Born in mystery!
Wakantanka shakes the sky.
Wakantanka shakes the sky.
Stars are falling.
Stars are falling.
Burning arrows from the sky.
Burning arrows from the sky.
Burning Arrow we will call him.
Burning Arrow we will call him.

That is how he came to be called Burning Arrow. This was his
mother-child-name, his name to grow on until he was nine winters old and received his father-child-name.

Suddenly missing the drumbeat of his mother's heart in the
place where he had sprung from his father's seed, in the place
where he had been growing and swimming for nine months, the
tiny one began to wail. Hapanna placed her hand firmly over his
mouth and gently pinched his nose to silence his cry.

Abhoo! Abhoo!
Hush, hush, my son.
The enemy will hear!
The enemy will hear!
Sleep, sleep, my son.

Hapanna took her newborn son to her own nearby *tipi* and her
own bed of buffalo robes, where she held him close to her heart
so that he could hear its drumbeat and be comforted. Winona,
her firstborn, her daughter, stirred in her bed and laughed in a
happy dream.

"My daughter," whispered Hapanna and smiled down at her.
"Someone will have wings on her heart when the sun rolls back
upon Mother Earth."

Confident that Wakantanka was still taking care of his two-
legged children, Uncida returned to her *tipi* and closed the flap
against intruders. She reverently hung her grandson's umbilical
cord to dry above the tiny fire under the smoke hole in her *tipi*.

12

She took out the two small turtle-shaped pouches she had made for this child-to-come's umbilical cord and had decorated with beads. Tomorrow she would stuff one with grass to fool the evil spirits. When the umbilical cord was dry, she would put it in the other pouch and sew it on her grandson's cradle until he could walk, when she would sew it on his clothes. It would be his guardian spirit while he toddled about and would keep him from falling into cooking fires or into the waters of the Lac qui Parle.

Still wakeful and full of wonder, Uncida placed a sweet smelling grass on the fire, breathed the sweet incense, and sat pondering this new man-child's time-to-come. Would his time-to-come trail the shooting stars? Was there some sacred meaning for him in this *wakan* night—this night of mystery? What would he choose to become when he was 14 winters old and took a man-name? Would he become a warrior like Strong Heart, his father? Would he become a hunter as Tunkasida, his grandfather, had been?

Uncida's heart was glad that the *wakan* mystery in the sky tonight was not the dread mystery, the flying mystery that streaked the black sky when the clouds made war cries. She did not want for this newborn that lightning mystery that sometimes visits a youth's sacred vision and makes him a *heyoka,* a contrary, a fool, a clown, the most difficult thing a Dakota youth could become. No, not that! Not a *heyoka,* who had to protect his Dakota band from the contrary *wakan* power in the sky—the *wakan* power that was not kind and trustworthy like the sun, the four winds, fire, flowing water, and growing plants. If *they* brought harm, it was your own fault. You had misused their kind power. But the ways of the thunder being that lived at the end of the world where the sun went down were different. He played tricks on people, sad and frightening tricks. When he opened his mouth, he spoke thunder. When he opened his eyes, lightning shot from them, and the lightning killed. The *heyoka* had to pray to the thunder being for the people, and his prayer had to speak in the contrary way the thunder being spoke. The *heyoka's* work was to play the contrary. The harder he prayed, the more contrary he acted, the more fool he was. In public he had to do and say everything backward. He had to do the normal things a person did in the

13

opposite way—even to walking on moccasinned hands, riding his horse backward, shivering in the summer heat, walking around in bitter cold wearing only his breechclout. Ah, no, not a *heyoka!* May her grandson never have to become a *heyoka,* the most difficult thing a Dakota man could be, even if his clowning gave his village the precious gift of laughter.

Perhaps, thought Uncida, perhaps my grandson in the time-to-come will be chosen to be one of Joseph Renville's soldier-guards. Perhaps he will be like his uncle-father Red Beaver and live in Tokandati, the great Soldier Lodge near the stockade. Perhaps Joseph Renville, who felt like a father to the Wahpetonwan Dakota band that had chosen to build their lodges near his fur-trading post, would look with pleased eyes at this grandson in the time-to-come and would invite him to be his bodyguard. If so, her grandson would go often to the meeting of the two big rivers and would see many white fur traders and white soldiers.

No, not that either! The white man was bad medicine. The white man brought new ways, destroying ways, ways that made Red Men throw out the old ways. Black cooking kettles that made Dakota women throw away their cooking sacs. Guns that took all the bravery out of killing the enemy and made it impossible for buffalo hunters to know their own kill. Blankets that did not have the wearing, staying power of buffalo skins. The spirit water that would surely destroy the Dakota villages' kinship way of life.

Had not she herself left Kaposia precisely because it was too close to the Long Knives' fort on the cliffs above the Minnesota? Even though Tunkasida's bones were buried near there? Even though she belonged to the Mdewakantonwan band of the Dakota nation, had she not used the Dakota privilege to choose and chosen to go with Winona and her son-in-law to live with the Wahpetonwans, many sleeps toward the setting sun? Other Mdewakantonwans had come to live at Lac qui Parle for the same reason and not simply because they were relatives of Joseph Renville's kind and beautiful full-blooded Mdewakantonwan wife, whom he had met at Kaposia and taken to Prairie du Chien to be married by a Black Robe.

14

Alone in her *tipi* while the sky rained stars, Uncida softly sang a prayer song for her grandson to all the good spirits, wherever they were—above, below, and all around:

> Earth Spirit, Sky Spirit,
> Spirit of the East, Spirit of the South,
> Spirit of the West, Spirit of the North,
> May my grandson walk the road of his grandfathers.
> May my grandson walk the Good Red Road.
> May my grandson never throw the drum away.
> May my grandson never break the sacred pipe.

When the sun rolled back onto the earth after that *wakan* night when the sky rained stars and the noon of night was as bright as the noon of day, Strong Heart and his brother Red Beaver and the warriors and counselors of the village came down from the ridge above the village on the Lac qui Parle where they had stood watch all night. Many of them had been sure that Grandfather Sun would never come back to them again. Thus there was a double joy in Strong Heart's voice when he took his newborn son in his arms and held him up to the rising sun.

> Grandfather, you have returned!
> The circle is not broken!
> Grandfather, behold my son!
> Give my son the keen eyes of the eagle.
> Give my son the strong arm of the bear.
> Give my son the swiftness of the deer.
>
> Grandfather, hear me!
> Make my son a true warrior.
> Make my son a defender of his people.
> Make my son an avenger of the slain.
>
> Grandfather, hear me!
> Make my son respect the ancient ways.
> Make my son respect his blood-relatives.
> Make my son respect his friend-relatives.
> Make my son respect his relatives the four-leggeds.

15

Make my son respect his winged relatives.
Make my son respect his little relatives in the grasses.
Make my son respect the waters and the hills.
Make my son respect the whole face of our Mother the
     Earth.

Mitakuya Owasin!
I am a relative to all!

While Strong Heart made his prayer for his son, Uncida quietly brought a bowl of hot rabbit soup to her daughter's tent for her son-in-law and quietly left again. While Strong Heart ate, Hapanna took her son to her breast. After that father and son slept most of the first day of Burning Arrow's life in the warm round *tipi* in the warm round ring of relatives by blood and by marriage and by Dakota kinship in the village on the banks of the Lac qui Parle.

2

The Corn Was
Plump with Milk

In spite of the torrential rain of stars on the night when Burning Arrow was born, the star nation the next night did not seem to be missing any stars. Grandmother Moon shone calmly down on the Lac qui Parle as if nothing strange at all had happened.

When Burning Arrow was as many sleeps old as the fingers on his two tiny hands, Grandfather Sun chose to shine most warmly on the honoring feast Strong Heart gave for his firstborn son. Uncida, Hapanna, and the aunts and cousins cooked many kettles of stew from the two deer Strong Heart and Red Beaver had shot the day before. The first to have their bowls filled were the very old and the very poor, and they were the first to receive gifts in the Give-Away. Following the ancient custom of the Dakotas, who believe that not to give freely and with a whole heart is to be less than human, Strong Heart gave gifts in honor of his son with glorious abandon—even his newest and finest buffalo robe that Hapanna and Uncida had scraped and made soft with a mixture of buffalo brain and liver. This gift Strong Heart gave to an old grandmother with deeply sunken cheeks.

"*Hi ho! Hi ho!*" exclaimed the guests in admiration.

"My son-in-law is a true Dakota," murmured Uncida to her heart, and her heart was glad.

Everybody's heart rejoiced because of the great honor that was being shown to the son of Strong Heart and Hapanna. More logs were thrown on the fire, and the circle of guests moved closer. Now the best storytellers began to tell their best stories. The loud-

17

est laughter was for a story Red Beaver had heard on his last journey with Joseph Renville to the Long Knives' fort. It had been told to him by a Mdewakantonwan who had traveled far down the Mississippi to a great white man's village.

"With his own eyes he saw a place where white men gave feasts *and asked their guests to pay,*" said Red Beaver.

"But that is not all," said Red Beaver, when the incredulous laughter had died down. "One white man feasted and walked away without paying, and the white policeman put irons on him and locked him up."

"Have they no pride?" wondered Uncida as she took Burning Arrow in his cradle to her *tipi* to change the cattail down. "To ask *pay* for a feast! To lock up a man and take away his freedom!"

Soon after the honoring feast and Give-Away, Grandmother Moon's face began to become winter-hard. A thin skin of ice began to grow on the edges of the lake. Most of the water birds that rested and fed on its waters in their flight to the waters that never freeze had come and gone. Wild rice and cranberries had been gathered and dried. The corn Joseph Renville had taught the Wahpetonwan village at his trading post to grow had been harvested and safely stored. The fall buffalo hunt was over. The staying snow would come any day now. The *tipis* in the Wahpetonwan village nestled close to the stockade glowed all night long with slow-burning, low-burning fires. The men-in-the-*tipi* time, the time when it was more comfortable to be inside than outside, had come. It was the time when a soup of jerk meat, dried prairie turnips, and dried corn simmered over many a cooking fire during the day. It was a time when men whose hair was white with many snows told the young whose hair was shiny and black as a crow's wing all that they knew. It was a time for telling deeds-of-valor stories, for gambling with plum stones, for playing the "Which moccasin has the plum stone?" game.

Burning Arrow quietly and gravely surveyed all this from his upright cradle, where he spent most of the first year of his life. Here he slept when he was sleepy. Here he played with the smooth small foot bones and toe bones Hapanna hung from the wooden bow which protected his face and head. Here he laughed at his sister Winona when she sang a song for each of his fingers.

18

Laced in the warm sack of this cradle, he rode on his mother's back when she walked the woman-worn path to the lake to get water. On another well-worn woman path he rode to the bottom-land where the women cut cottonwood that left no smoke taste in the food. On another mother-worn path he rode to the cattail swamp where Hapanna gathered fresh fluff to replace the wet soiled fluff in his pouch. From the Moon of Popping Trees to the Moon of Snow Blindness Hapanna rubbed charcoal-blackened bear fat into Burning Arrow's and Winona's cheeks to protect them from having frosted cheeks and eyes. Wisely, she did not keep them inside the *tipi* all winter long, for they must learn to know the cold that bites and must become toughened to face the cold that kills.

When Strong Heart was gone hunting or through-the-ice fishing, Uncida sat in her daughter's *tipi* and helped Hapanna make big and little garments and moccasins and decorate them with brightly dyed porcupine quills. With her old-but-still-nimble fingers she sewed and mended, and while she worked she sang brave-heart songs to Burning Arrow so that he would not grow up to be a coward. If he became fretful, she sang calming songs.

Shuh . . . shhuh!
Shuh . . . shhuh!
Sleep, my grandson.
Sleep, sleep, sleep!
The enemy is far away,
is far away!

But when Uncida heard the soft thud of a small-animal body against the *tipi*, she knew that Strong Heart had returned from the hunt. Quickly she covered her face with her blanket and returned to her own *tipi*, where more often than not she found lying before her own door a snowshoe rabbit or a fish. Because of an ancient custom, a daughter's husband was a relative to be avoided. Mothers-in-law and sons-in-law must avoid direct meeting, direct speaking, direct looking at each other. The same custom held for fathers-in-law and daughters-in-law, but not for a grandparent and grandchildren. Uncida could talk freely and fondly with Burning Arrow as long as she lived. The grandmother's privilege was greater even than a sister's. After eight or nine winters another ancient custom would keep Winona and Burning Arrow from direct conversation—a strange custom, but perhaps not so strange. It showed how determined the ancient grandfathers were that a Dakota boy grow up and be a true Dakota man with a fearless heart.

Inside Hapanna's *tipi* Burning Arrow watched with bright eyes while his mother took off his father's wet moccasins, rubbed his cold feet between her hands, and put dry moccasins on him.

"Ho! New!" exclaimed Strong Heart approvingly. "My wife is good to her husband."

"My husband is good to his woman," murmured Hapanna, placing a willow-rod lean-back in his place of honor at the back of the *tipi*, at the left and heart-side of the *tipi*-home.

When Burning Arrow was five moons old, the water birds began to come back and build their nests. Once again the red-tailed hawks rode the west wind high in the sky above Lac qui Parle. When the baby birds were hatching and the parent birds that cry "Tee-bdo! Tee-bdo!" were anxiously following their scampering, scattering young, Uncida and Hapanna joined the other women of the village in the planting of the corn. Burning Arrow's cradle was propped against a boulder, and Winona was stationed at his side to scare away the flies and brush away the insects that stab and raise bumps. When Hapanna stopped her work to give her breast to Burning Arrow, Winona followed Uncida and dropped the sprouted corn kernels in the holes her grandmother dug for them in the rich mellow ground where the wild artichokes liked to grow. Later, in the Moon When the Strawberries Are Red, while the women hoed the corn, Winona brought Burning Arrow fistfuls of strawberries still on their stems and fed them to him one by one.

In the Moon of Chokecherries, Burning Arrow saw a *heyoka* dance for the first time. It was a good day for corn to grow, a good day for children who did not have to guard the corn against the blackbirds to play water games in the lake, but a hot day for women working and for men hunting. When the day was getting old and older, storm clouds piled into black hills where the sky in the west rubbed against Mother Earth and advanced with frightening flash and noise. When the first rush of wind bent the trees on the ridge across the Lac qui Parle, the *heyoka*, who went about all summer huddled in his blanket and shivering with cold, danced on moccasinned hands around the circle of lodges. Burning Arrow thought it was antic play to make him glad and laughed aloud. A fork of lightning struck the ridge across the lake, followed quickly by a crash of thunder so loud that Hapanna snatched Burning Arrow to her heart and clasped Winona's hand tightly.

"*Heyoka* dances for our good," she said to him. "He asks the thunder being not to hurl his flying mystery at us."

By the time the corn was as plump with milk as his mother's breast, Burning Arrow as good as leaped from his cradle and refused to be put back. Naked as the night he was born, he toddled about the Wahpetonwan village and was welcomed at any and at every *tipi*. For Burning Arrow was not born into a single family but into a great kinship family where everyone was a relative. His father's and mother's relatives were his blood-mothers, blood-fathers, blood-brothers, and blood-sisters. But others were *hunka*-relatives, friend-relatives, relatives-by-choice. And *hunka*-relatives were just as good as blood-relatives!

Big-brother-arms scooped Burning Arrow up to broad shoulders, where he grabbed long black braids or hanks of sleek black hair and hung on tightly for a rough child-horse ride. One golden autumn day his roughriding horse was his uncle-father, Red Beaver, who galloped him into Renville's stockade and into the great hall with a fireplace so large that it burned logs upended. There he played for a time with Jean Baptiste, the youngest of Joseph Renville's eight children.

Renville sat silent for a time watching Burning Arrow trying to catch Jean Baptiste, *Koda Mitawa*, his pet lamb. "Who knows what the future holds for these two," he sighed to Red Beaver. It was a sigh from the ribs under his heart. "I see many changes in the time to come, and some, I fear, are not so good!"

3

The New Moon Has Two Horns

Every spring, as soon as the rivers and creeks had gone back to their banks and the prairies had lost their snow-water wetness, Joseph Renville took the winter's harvest of hides to Henry Sibley, the Long Trader, at the meeting of the two great rivers. The Wahpetonwan village hummed with excitement on the day when the ox carts, loaded with smelly hides, and the Renville family, accompanied by 50 or 60 Dakota and half-breeds, followed the rutted trail toward the rising sun. Burning Arrow's uncle-father Red Beaver and other soldier-guards rode ahead and behind and alongside the wagon train, on constant watch for the enemy. Since the noise of the wheels, the screeching of wood on wood, could be heard for miles, this journey could not be kept from enemy ears.

Since Joseph Renville had nothing but kind thoughts in his heart for all Indians, be they Dakota, Ojibway, Sac, or Fox, it was a thing to wonder that anyone would wish to harm him. His kind hospitality to Indians and whites was known up and down all the rivers that flowed into the Father of Waters. What white explorer, what Indian chief had not feasted on bear meat, venison, antelope, buffalo, turnips, potatoes, wild rice, corn, and maple sugar at Joseph Renville's table! Only someone whose body had become the home of an evil spirit could wish to do harm to Joseph Renville!

Ah, but Joseph Renville had Dakota blood! He was a son of a French trader and a woman of the Mdewakantonwan band at

22

Kaposia. Joseph Renville's wife was a full-blooded Dakota of the same band. His children had Dakota blood. Their scalps would bring glory to the enemy, be they Ojibway, Sac, or Fox. Moreover, Joseph Renville loved his wife and children as dearly as he loved himself and wanted no harm to come to them.

More exciting even than the annual spring departure of the wagon train was its return. Renville took his time, for there were so many old friends to visit: Henry Sibley; Major Laurence Taliaferro, the Indian agent who was so fair to the Indians that some of the fur traders wished that he would be sent somewhere else; Majors Bliss and Loomis at the Fort; and the band of relatives at Kaposia, Little Crow's village, where there was much feasting and dancing in their honor and at least one rough and rollicking game of lacrosse with a neighboring band. Two new moons could grow fat and full and be nibbled away before the watchers on the hills above the Lac qui Parle, constantly scanning the lake and the prairies for enemy from the south or from the north, saw the wagon train in the distance. When they saw the train of Renville's 50 Red River carts beginning to cross the Mayawakan River about five miles from the village, they sent a runner to carry the news.

"*Ee-Ho! Ee-Ho!* They come! They come!"

Women dropped their work and children their play. Old men and women who could scarcely walk joined the crowd of people and dogs streaming to meet relatives and *hunka*-relatives returning from a great adventure. What news would they bring? What amazing new things from the white men's trading posts? There were those such as Uncida and Strong Heart who scorned the white men's things and thought that they were destroying the old ways. But what Dakota woman would give up the white man's iron kettle to go back to boiling meat by dropping fist-sized heated stones into a buffalo paunch of water? What woman preferred the hard work of scraping a fresh hide and making it mellow-soft for garments to buying the white man's bright calico? Indeed, what Dakota warrior or hunter did not hanker for a white man's gun, if he did not already have one? After all, a gun kills from ten times as far away as an arrow!

But the white men's new thing that came back with Joseph

23

Renville and arrived on July 9, 1835, was so unlike the other new things that found their way to this remote post on the upper Minnesota that the Wahpetonwan band was quite unprepared for it. For the time being the meaning of the new thing hid itself from their hearts.

"It came like a snake in the grass," some said later.

"Like the covered embers for a new campfire," said others.

The new thing was a small band of white people: two faces-full-of-hair men, three women in long ugly dresses and hiding-hair bonnets, two children dressed like tiny grandparents—tiny white grandparents. The Wahpetonwan mothers threw pitying sounds at them, for it was a day when the sun blazed in a cloudless sky and the prairie shimmered with heat. But, true to Dakota etiquette, they guarded their eyes and did not rudely stare. Nor would they have asked prying questions of them if they could have spoken their language. The questions came later when the cool evening breezes had risen and the white-fire insects were flying and Red Beaver had come to smoke with Strong Heart and his relatives. The women and children sat in a circle behind the men, the women listening eagerly, the children dropping off to sleep one by one.

The pipe went the full circle of men before anyone spoke.

"My younger brother, our hearts are glad that you have returned," said Strong Heart at last.

"*Ho Hay!*" agreed the men-relatives, and the women murmured a soft tremolo of assent.

"My younger brother, our eyes see that Joseph Renville has brought visitors. Other white visitors have come and gone. These visitors have the staying look. They have brought their women and children. Our hearts are wondering and asking why?"

Red Beaver drew four long draughts of fragrant smoke, puffed it slowly into the air, and started the pipe around the circle again.

"The man who is called Huggins is a man who plants," said Red Beaver. "Joseph Renville invited him to our village to teach us to farm the white man's way. He wishes to protect us against the times when our children cry and our old men and women die with hunger. The man who is called Williamson is a man of prayer and also a medicine man. Joseph Renville has invited him

24

here to teach us the white man's Spirit Law, to teach us to read the white man's Spirit Law that is written in the white man's Sacred Book. Many snows and grasses ago Joseph Renville had a French trader bring him the Sacred Book from across the Salt Waters. I myself have heard someone read from the Sacred Book to Joseph Renville. Joseph Renville's heart finds the teaching in the white man's Sacred Book good. The words in the white man's Sacred Book go as sunlight to his heart. He wants his own children to learn to read and to write those words. Joseph Renville wants the soldier-guards of the Tokandati Lodge to learn to read and to write those words. He wants his Dakota brothers and sisters to learn to read and to write those words."

After Red Beaver had stopped speaking there was a long silence, followed by some few murmurs of approval but mostly of disapproval. But before Strong Heart collected all the feelings of disapproval into strong words and spoke them, an old close-relative who had never camped near the white men's Soldier Lodge near the meeting of the two rivers asked the seeking question nosing in his heart. "My grandson, what is it to *read* and to *write?*"

"My grandfather," answered Red Beaver, "the white man has books with talking leaves. The white man has talking sticks. The white man touches his talking stick to the talking leaves and places the thoughts of his heart upon the leaves. It is a silent talking. Joseph Renville wants his children, his soldier warriors, and his Dakota brothers and sisters to learn the silent talking of the talking leaves. Joseph Renville says clouds of change are gathering. He says books are the white man's bows and arrows. He says his Dakota brothers must learn to use the white man's bows and arrows."

"My younger brother," Strong Heart began softly, and there was fondness for Red Beaver his blood-brother in his voice, but his voice quickly spoke his scorn for what Red Beaver had spoken. "Can the white man's books with the talking leaves kill an enemy? Can the white man's talking stick shoot a buffalo? Can the white man's talking leaves talk Dakota?"

"*Ho Hay! Ho Hay!*" shouted the men-relatives with such loud approval that Burning Arrow was startled from his sleep.

"No, my younger brother," continued Strong Heart, his voice dropping to softness again, "Dakota men do not need a new trail. Dakota men do not want the white man's trail or his Sacred Book. If the Great Mystery had wanted Dakota men to have a Sacred Book, why did he give it to the white men and not to Dakota men?"

Before he dropped back to sleep again on Hapanna's lap, Burning Arrow looked up at the shiny canoe in the great lake of the sky. He saw and yet did not see that the new moon not only looked like a birchbark canoe but also like two horns growing on the head of a hoofed four-legged relative.

4

The Fork in the Trail

"My younger brother, is your heart walking away from the Dakota trail?" Strong Heart asked Red Beaver one day after the latter began going to the school the missionary-doctor started almost at once in the Tokandati Soldier Lodge.

"My elder brother," answered Red Beaver gently. "Did not our grandfather tell us that when a good Dakota sees a footprint or a new trail he follows it until he knows what it is, until he knows if it is good or not? To open the ears does not mean to open the heart."

Most of the Dakota men in the Wahpetonwan village on the Lac qui Parle took the wait-and-see attitude toward the new thing the white missionaries brought. Not all were as willing to open their ears as was Red Beaver, nor as eager to scout the new trail as was Eagle Help.

Perhaps Eagle Help was eager to learn from the missionary-doctor because both were medicine men and spirit men at the same time. Dr. Williamson knew the secrets of the white men's medicine. Eagle Help knew the secrets of Mother Earth's medicine. He knew the healing power of roots and leaves, of grasses and flowers. He knew what to boil to cure stomach pains and backaches. He knew what would heal sores and stop bleeding, what would stop and unstop bowels. Dr. Williamson had *wakan* knowledge of the white man's god and son-of-god and of the white man's Sacred Book. Eagle Help also had *wakan* knowledge and experienced mysteries not given to ordinary men. He could

27

fast and see visions that revealed exactly where to find the enemy. No war party ever went out of the village without first consulting Eagle Help.

Burning Arrow's father had the highest respect for Eagle Help. Thus he was both surprised and displeased when Red Beaver came to Hapanna's *tipi* one night and reported that Eagle Help was the first of them to learn to read and to write the Dakota language.

"My younger brother, can the white man teach something he does not know?" asked Strong Heart. "The white man does not know the language of the Dakota any more than he knows the language of the winged ones that fly in the sky or the four-leggeds who walk on the earth or the tiny ones who hum and creep in the grass. Can the missionary-doctor put dog words upon the talking leaves? The Dakota are Mother Earth's children, and their language cannot be put on the white man's talking leaves."

Red Beaver explained to them how Joseph Renville was helping the missionary-doctor put the meanings of Dakota words into signs and symbols that could in truth be written down—on talking leaves, on the back of the white man's shovel, in ashes scattered on the floor. "Joseph Renville has his son, Jean Baptiste, run to him. '*In-yan-ka*,' Joseph Renville says slowly and clearly. 'The boy runs.' '*In-yan-ka*,' Dr. Williamson repeats slowly and clearly after him. 'The boy runs.' '*Hecetu!* That is right!' says Joseph Renville. Dr. Williamson touches his talking stick and speaks the Dakota meaning to the talking leaves."

"Eagle Help has now learned the signs and symbols," said Red Beaver. "This very day Dr. Williamson wrote something in big signs and symbols, and Eagle Help spoke the message to all ears. The talking leaves spoke Dakota to Eagle Help's eyes, and his tongue spoke the message in Dakota correctly."

"*Hu Hee!*" exclaimed Hapanna in amazement, and Burning Arrow, who was having his last meal of the day at her breast, raised his head and looked a quiet why into her eyes.

"What was the message, my younger brother?" asked Strong Heart.

"We bring you the straight path of the one true god," Red Beaver replied.

28

"My younger brother, the message lies!" said Strong Heart harshly.

"My elder brother," said Red Beaver quietly. "I will wait and see."

But Hapanna and some of the other women in the Wahpeton-wan village did not wait long to choose the true god-and-son-of-god way. In the beginning not one full-blooded Dakota man chose to go that way. About 20 of them had gone to the first meeting in one of Joseph Renville's log houses inside the stockade, where the two missionary families lived until they had built their own lodge. The Dakota men had sat cross-legged on the earthen floor while the women and children listened at the windows. The missionary-doctor had told them the story of the great god who loved his earth children—all his earth children, white, red, brown, and black—loved them so much that he sent his only son Jesus Christ to earth. Even though Joseph Renville had helped the missionary-doctor prepare the story, the telling was full of mistakes. Yet the Dakota audience listened quietly, respectfully, and did not smile. If they thought it strange that the speaker never paused to let his listeners make approving or disapproving sounds, their faces did not tell the speaker so. Later, of course, when they smoked among themselves, they said their laughing and scorning thoughts to each other.

"Where is this great god? Up in the sky? In the clouds? Behind the moon? At the end of the Spirit Trail?"

"My brothers, have you ever seen the little path that leads to the great god's home in the sky?"

"Is the son of god a hairy white man or a clean barefaced redman?"

"Could the son of god kill two buffalo with one arrow?"

"What son of a Dakota man would bring such shame to his father? Surely the son of god must have had a rabbit heart to let himself be killed by the enemy instead of dying gloriously in battle!"

It was some of the Dakota women who went back to hear more about this son of god who seemed to have a heart as tender as a tender woman heart. They went inside the log lodge and sat on the earthern floor, their legs discreetly pointing left, their eyes modestly turned downward while the missionary-doctor spoke in fumbling, stumbling Dakota.

Now every white man's holy day Hapanna combed Winona's and her own hair, black and shiny with oil, and braided it neatly. They put their brightest and best blankets over their shoulders and went to the white missionary's lodge to pray and to sing to the white man's great god. Winona, bursting with all the new things she saw and heard, told them to Burning Arrow and Uncida. Burning Arrow could not go along because Strong Heart, his father, would not let him. Uncida would not go along because her heart would not let her.

The summer grew very old, and the staying snows came. In the year and the moon when a *wakan* light streaked across the night sky, a son was born to the wife of the missionary-doctor. On the holy day when the new son received his name and had the saving waters poured on his head, Winona came home from the missionary lodge and went straight to Uncida's *tipi* to tell all that she had seen and heard. Uncida stopped singing the brave-heart songs she was singing to Burning Arrow to help him grow up to be a great Dakota warrior and listened quietly.

"Uncida, he is so tiny! And his face is red and wrinkled like my little brother's when he was born, but my mother says it will soon get pale. His name is John—John Poage Williamson. I don't know what it means, but I think it means Someone-who-loves-Jesus. They said his name and poured the saving waters on his head and said things in their language I could not understand. My mother says that some day she and I will have new names and will have the saving waters poured on our heads. She wishes my little brother could get a new name and have the saving waters poured on his head!"

The lines that flowed like rivers from Uncida's eyes and most of the time smiled and laughed became set and hard. "If my daughter who is called Hapanna and my granddaughter who is called Winona take a saving-waters name they will no longer be Dakota," she said. "They will leave the Good Red Road and go on the White Man's Road. If Wakantanka's red children take the White Man's Road, Wakantanka will be angry with them and they will die."

30

When Winona began to cry, Uncida became so distressed that she asked a turning-around question. "Did the white father give a naming feast for his son, and did they have a Give-Away, and did they dance?"

"Oh, no, Uncida," sobbed Winona. "The great god says it is bad to dance."

"Bad to dance!" exclaimed Uncida. "When we Dakota dance we are at our very best! When we Dakota dance we are most Dakota!"

When Burning Arrow heard the word dance, his black eyes sparkled. But two winters old, he already knew the joy he felt when the village danced. His heart ears could even now hear the low, wild drumming of drums, the hard pound-pound of the men's feet, the softer shuffle-shuffle of the women's feet, the patter-patter of the children's feet, the rattle-rattle of clicking knee rattles and arm rattles, pebble rattles in the gourds. His heart eyes could see the warriors whirling, whirling in the dance, their naked bodies gleaming with paint.

"*Waci! Waci!* Dance! Dance!" he cried, wriggling from Uncida's arms. Uncida watched Burning Arrow dancing around her *tipi* fire, and the hard lines on her face turned soft again with laughter.

5

Every New Day
Is *Wakan*

Very early in his life Burning Arrow learned to know other joys
as well as the joy of the dances. He knew the day would hold
excitement when he heard the village crier call: "Men! Women!
Open your ears! Get ready to move! Men, prepare the hunting
weapons. Women, prepare to pack the dog drags and the pony
drags. Prepare to take down the *tipis*. At the rising of the sun
we go to hunt." A camping trip. Maybe a hunting of the buffalo
on the prairie toward the setting sun. Maybe a hunting of the
white-tailed timber deer in the woodlands toward the rising sun.
Or a camping in a grove of sweet-juice trees and feasting on
maple sugar. Or a harvesting of wild rice on one of the lakes in
the direction of the enemy.

When Burning Arrow's ears heard the *"Weh! Weh! Weh!"*
call of the women collecting the dogs to pull the dog drags, his
heart drummed fast with joy. It meant a long and wild and
bouncy ride behind a dog or a pony. But he found it even more
fun when he was old enough to run with the pack of children
in the long caravan traveling to a new camp. Winona had to
carry a bundle bigger than her little woman-child self. No carrying of burdens for Burning Arrow. He was a child-man, and
Dakota men carried nothing but their weapons of hunt or of war.

Burning Arrow already carried his warrior weapon—a toy bow
of willow wood and blunted arrows Strong Heart had made for
him the winter after he was born. His father and father-uncle
taught him to carry his bow and arrow even when he went to

wet the grass in the place where Dakota males went to wet the grass or squat in it.

One day Burning Arrow and his playmates attacked a hornets' nest with their bows and arrows. They lost the battle and fled to their mothers' *tipis* with their many wounds. While Hapanna rubbed the minty juice from the crushed leaves of the heal-all flower on his hornet stings, Burning Arrow asked his father why Wakantanka, the Great Mystery who had made everything, had made hornets.

"To be the enemies of small boys and to train them to be brave warriors and not cry, my son. To teach them not to fear the enemy. To teach them not to fear the Ojibways."

"Why did Wakantanka make the Ojibways?"

"To be our enemies."

"Why are they our enemies?" asked Burning Arrow.

Strong Heart could not answer, for Strong Heart could not remember. In fact, not even the oldest grandfather in the Wahpetonwan Dakota village on the Lac qui Parle could send his memories back so far as to see the very first time Ojibways and Dakotas first shed each other's blood. Remember they could not, but every Dakota man, woman, and child knew that every Ojibway man, woman, and child was an enemy—a born enemy. From their first breath of life to their last, a Dakota and an Ojibway were enemies.

When breath made white smoke and the circle of cone-shaped *tipis* glowed mellow-yellow in the dark, Burning Arrow lay on his buffalo-hide bed and listened to the deeds-of-valor stories his father and father-uncles and *hunka*-uncles told. He learned to know the story for each golden eagle or common eagle feather his father and uncles wore on their heads. He fell asleep listening to the stories, dreamed of surprise attacks, and sometimes tossed wildly in his sleep.

"Shuh . . . shhuh, my son! Shuh . . . shhuh!" crooned Hapanna, tucking the buffalo robe around him. "The Ojibway are far away."

Burning Arrow began to day-dream, wake-dream of doing brave deeds and of making himself glory. Maybe, even if he was only a little boy, maybe he could surprise an enemy and kill

33

him with his bow and arrow and earn the right to wear the feather of a golden eagle!

The stories his father and uncles told and the songs they sang made Burning Arrow feel big and brave inside and out and all over. They made his heart feel strong as a grizzly bear.

The stories that Uncida and Hapanna told and the songs they sang made Burning Arrow and Winona feel brother and sister to everything Wakantanka had made—except, of course, the enemy. From Uncida and Hapanna they did not hear deeds-of-glory stories but beginning-stories.

"Everything has a beginning," said Uncida. "Everything has a story to tell. The tiniest bug crawling in the grass has a story to tell."

Because Uncida believed that everything had a story, she believed that everything could speak. Indeed, everything did seem to speak to her—even stones. Uncida never said, "If only stones could speak!" Uncida often said, "Stones are the firstborn, the great-great-grandfathers. They know the time before. They alone will know the time to come. Listen to the spirit of the stones."

So Burning Arrow began to listen to stones, of which there were plenty in and around the Lac qui Parle. Some of them were wild-rose pink, like the ribbons the sun flung out when it climbed back on earth at dawn. It would not have surprised Burning Arrow one bit if a pink stone had opened its mouth to speak to him.

Because Uncida believed that everything could speak to her, she believed that everything could hear her speak. She told the Minnesota River that flowed through Lac qui Parle and made a big bend on its way to the Father of Waters what a beautiful river it was. She sang to the butterflies and the dragonflies, to a whitetail deer and its twin spotted fawns, to the rabbit and fox. She spoke to the Spirit Path, the Milky Way, leading to the Old Grandfathers beyond the stars.

When very early—unusually early!—in his life small thoughts began to awaken in Burning Arrow's heart like birds beginning to trill just before sunrise, it was only natural for him to go to Uncida with them. By now he had learned how to be a good relative. He already knew the right kinship words for each relative and had

34

learned never to ask intrusive questions. Like every other Dakota child, he had but one fear—to be rebuked for boldness. Yet troubled whys began to creep into his mind, questions he could not ask with a simple why. And the questions refused to leave without an answer. There was nothing to do but go to Uncida. Even if she told him again and again, "Be a good Dakota, my grandson," he somehow knew that she would not say, "Do not ask that question. A good Dakota boy never does so!"

When trouble came into Hapanna's *tipi* because she would not work or let Winona work or play on the white man's holy day, Burning Arrow went to Uncida's *tipi* and asked questions like this:

"Why does the white missionary-doctor say that it is bad to play ball on the holy day?"

"Why is it bad to work on the holy day?"

"If the seventh day is holy, can the white man do as he pleases on the other six days?"

"My grandson," said Uncida, "when you were born on the *wakan* night when the sky rained stars, I think that you shot like a burning arrow through the horns of the new moon."

Uncida had gone to the Land of the Spirits before Burning Arrow fully understood what she meant when she said that riddle thing about him. By that time his small thoughts had become man thoughts, and he did not let them chatter like blackbirds in the spring. By that time he also understood that what his grandmother spoke to his small thoughts was like a great secret hidden in a nutshell.

"Every new day is *wakan,* a sacred day," Uncida told Burning Arrow. "Every new day is a *wakan* event. Every day Grandfather Wakantanka sends us his *wakan* light and every day we thank him for doing it again."

Burning Arrow was troubled again on that holy day when Hapanna and Winona had the saving waters poured on their heads and solemnly renounced all trust in "stones and earth and sky and all their hosts" and promised to trust alone "in the true and living God." They also received new names. Now the white people and the few baptized Wahpetonwan women called Hapanna Sarah, and Winona Julia.

On the white man's holy day when this took place, Burning Arrow ran swiftly to Uncida, who was hoeing corn. "My grandmother, never, never will I call my mother Sarah and my sister Julia!" he sputtered. Then in a small-boy whimpering voice he asked Uncida why. Why did his father let this bad thing happen? Why did his father not put a stop to this bad thing?

Uncida was glad to sit under a cottonwood and answer her grandson's questions. What was the joy of helping the tender green plants grow up to the joy of helping tender green thought-lings grow up?

"Why?" asked Burning Arrow.

Uncida did not answer at once but began to sing in a low voice.

> It is good to sit quietly.
> It is good to sit quietly.
> No talking.
> No talking.
> It is good to sit quietly.

A killdeer plaintively scolded her young ones, scampering to the sparkling water of the Lac qui Parle. A red-tailed hawk landed on a pink rock in the lake.

"My grandson," said Uncida at last, "a good Dakota wife, a good Dakota mother rules the *tipi*. Our Mother Earth made it so. So it is with our Sister Bear, our Sister Deer. My daughter, your mother, is a good wife, a good mother. She dresses the skins my son-in-law, your father, takes in the hunt. She makes garments for her children. She cures the bark of the red willow, the kinnikinnik, for tobacco. She grinds the corn until none is finer. She weaves baskets of grass for ripe berries. She cooks the wild rice and the meat dishes, and her heart is glad to feed her guests. She searches the hearts of her husband, her children, and her guests to save them the trouble of talking. My daughter, your mother, is a good wife, a good mother. My son-in-law, your father, loves and trusts her. If she wishes to search out a new way, she is free to do so. A Dakota is free. There is nothing freer than a Dakota."

"But will Wakantanka become angry with her and turn his back on her?" Burning Arrow asked.

"Wakantanka is a good grandfather. A good grandfather loves his grandchildren and smiles at whatever they do. After all, they are only children."

Burning Arrow became very sober. "The white man's great god is not like that. My sister says that if we do not have the saving waters poured on our heads he will send us to a bad place where we will burn and burn and never burn up. My sister begs me to have the saving waters poured on my head so that I will go to the white man's Spirit Land with her. What does your heart say about that, Uncida?"

"My grandchild," said Uncida softly. "Tunkasida, your grandfather, is already in the Dakota Land of Spirits. I want to be with him. I do not want to go to the white man's Spirit Land if Tunkasida is not there."

"I do not want to go there either," said Burning Arrow firmly.

But why thoughts promptly crept into his mind again. Why could they not *all* be there together in one big happy family, all of them sitting around cooking fires in a great Ring of Spirits at the end of the Spirit Path?

6

Of Happy Things and Curious Things and an Evil Thing

The summer when he was almost four winters old may well have been the happiest summer in Burning Arrow's life. For him the moon that summer seemed always fat and full. As yet he did not know the skinny moon of hunger and hardship, of troubles with the white men. Every morning Hapanna filled his wooden bowl with something steaming and good. After that his day was play. Although he was very young, he was adopted into Jean Baptiste Renville's band of boys who still slept on the mother-side of the *tipi* and had not yet moved to the left and father-side. For the time being they could play at war and not be sternly disciplined and trained by fathers and father-uncles to follow the real warpath. They could race and wrestle, swim and play water games. They could shoot their blunted arrows into braided grass targets. They could fight mock battles with pretend enemies and real battles with each other, slinging mud balls from the tips of slender, springy willows.

One of their favorite sports that summer was racing down the southern slopes, crossing the deep ravine, and climbing to the hillside sloping to the lower end of the Lac qui Parle. Here the missionary band now lived in their own log lodge. Here they now had their school and their meetings. Here there was always something curious for inquisitive Dakota boys to see and to hear —Dakota boys who never went to the missionary meetings.

One of these journeys was to satisfy their curiosity that the story Jean Baptiste had told them was a true-story and not a tease-story. Jean Baptiste, who went along with his family to the missionary's log lodge every holy day, had told them that the missionary-doctor Williamson had built his log lodge around a huge flat stone. There was a little hollow in the stone into which little John Williamson poured milk for his pet. Peering through the window and the open door, the boys saw with their own eyes that all this was true. In fact, little John Williamson brought his pet out to them and let each one hold it. Such a pet as this they had never before seen. Pets they had, of course. They had tamed fox kittens, bear cubs, wolf puppies, spotted fawns, buffalo calves, raccoon babies, all kinds of birds, but they had never tamed a spitting wildcat. This little four-legged, this little cat that sang a humming song when they stroked it, was a new and marvel-thing to them.

"In what manner do they say of you?" Burning Arrow asked the little creature when it was his turn to hold it.

"Kitty," said Little John Williamson promptly.

"Kee-tee," repeated Burning Arrow and wonderingly held the new four-legged up to his ear and listened to its humming song. Did "Kee-tee" perhaps mean "She who sings a humming song" in the white man's tongue?

Burning Arrow and his friends watched the white man's oxen plod round and round and round and turn the millstones that had been brought from the homeland of the missionaries. They marveled at the white man's mill that could crush and grind more wheat before the sun reached the middle of the sky than their mothers could grind in a moon.

Most curious of all was the sight of the missionary men doing the work of women. There were three white men now since Gideon Pond had come for a long stay. He had come from Cloudman's village near the Soldier Lodge at the meeting of the rivers. To the Dakota boys' unbelieving eyes Gideon Pond, Farmer Huggins, and the missionary-doctor Williamson carried buckets of water from the spring up the steep ridge, cut trees, carried wood, plowed the garden, made a split-rail fence around the garden, and planted corn, potatoes, oats, flax, wheat, and turnips. Woman-work! All of it!

On this particular day the three white men were hoeing the garden.

"They are not men!" snorted Gray Sparrow, one of Burning Arrow's cousins. "They should wear skirts."

"They do woman-work," agreed Lives-with-his-Grandmother, "but the white doctor made my grandmother's fever go away. My grandmother says that he has the heart of an Indian."

"See, he walks in Indian moccasins," said Burning Arrow, who also remembered a day not so long ago when he had gorged on maple sugar and lay in misery, sure that the spirits of dog and panther were fighting a battle in his stomach. His father had sent for Eagle Help, and his mother had sent Winona to get the missionary-doctor. The white doctor had come and stood quietly and watched the Dakota doctor swiftly pour a powder from his medicine bag into a bowl of water, mix it, and give it to Burning Arrow to drink.

When Hapanna begged him to give her son white men's medicine the missionary-doctor had smiled and shaken his head. "Eagle Help's medicine is good. It will cure your son swiftly and well."

And so it had!

It was Jean Baptiste who boasted of even more curious things taking place in his father's great hall with a fireplace so large it burned logs upended. "My father," boasted Jean Baptiste, "has a Sacred Book as old as the times when our grandfathers were canoe people and hunted in the land of many waters."

"*Hiwo!*" snorted Gray Sparrow, who was a born tease. "How did he get it? Did it fall from the sky?"

"My father had a French trader bring it to him from across the Salt Waters," answered Jean Baptiste. "And now Gideon Pond and the missionary-doctor are helping my father make the Sacred Book that speaks French speak Dakota."

"*Hiwo!*" teased Gray Sparrow. "Are you sure that you are not talking like a *heyoka?* Are you sure it is not the other way around? Your father is helping Gideon Pond and the missionary-doctor?"

"The missionary-doctor Williamson reads what the Sacred Book speaks in French. My father listens. Then my father speaks what the Sacred Book says in the Dakota language. Gideon Pond sits at a table and writes it on the talking leaves. It is my father who tells Pond what to write."

When Burning Arrow asked his father-uncle Red Beaver if this were really so, Red Beaver told him that this was indeed the way it was. After all, he ought to know, for he was Joseph Renville's soldier-guard and sat with the other soldier-guards on the long benches along the wall, guarding Renville, his family, and the village. As a matter of fact, guarding the missionaries, too!

If that summer was good, the autumn was even better. Only once did it not seem so—the brief time Burning Arrow feared that he would have to go along with Winona to the mission school. He lay in bed one night listening to his mother plead with his father in a low voice. When his father said that the white man's school was for women only—for Rosaline, Magdaline, and Margaret Renville, for child-women like Winona, Rda, and Rota, his mother answered, "Eagle Help's sons go. Jean Baptiste goes. Zitkadan goes. Catan and Hepidan go."

"Not my son!" interrupted Strong Heart harshly. "My son will not learn to read the white man's books. My son will learn to read our Mother Earth's book. My son will learn the sign language she writes for her Dakota children in the air, on the ground, in bushes and trees. The cloud signs, the sun-blood-red-going-down signs. The bark of the tree signs. The dew on the grass signs. My son will learn to read the Dakota signs. To know an enemy footprint by the shape of the moccasin. To read the secret signs Dakota braves leave for brother-friends on their far journeys. This my son will learn to read!"

When the bittersweet and sumac began to flame and the wild grape vines turned red, another mission family came to the Lac qui Parle mission. And in the same moon in which Burning Arrow and John Williamson had been born two winters apart, Gideon Pond married the schoolteacher, Miss Sarah Poage. Everyone in the village was invited, and many an old Dakota woman and man who had refused to come to the holy day worship came to the wedding and the feast afterwards. Gideon Pond had invited them personally, and he personally saw to it that their bowls were filled again and again with a tender soup of beef, potatoes, and turnips.

41

The most exciting event after that in the Wahpetonwan village on the Lac qui Parle was the passing through of the great train of ox carts from the Red River settlement on its way to Fort Snelling at the end of that moon and its return at the end of the next moon, bearing supplies for the long, long winter.

And long it was—that winter! The corn, dried buffalo meat, and wild rice were all eaten up by the time the cottonwoods along the lake shore began to show faint green. A hunting party of six Wahpetonwan families decided to trap and hunt for two weeks on the upper part of the Mayawakan River that flowed into the Minnesota below Fort Renville. If Hapanna had been willing to work on the holy day, Burning Arrow's family would have gone along and there would have been seven families.

"My *hunka*-brother," said one of Strong Heart's friends, "why do you not beat your wife?"

Strong Heart was quite sure that not even a beating would change Hapanna's heart about breaking the Spirit Law that said no one should work or play on the seventh day. But it was the love in his heart for Hapanna, stronger than his anger, that made him not beat her or try in any way to make her bend to his will.

To no one's surprise Gideon Pond went along with the six families. By this time the Dakota in the village on the Lac qui Parle knew that he was their brother under his white skin and big black beard. The hunting party welcomed his company, assuring him that on his holy day they would let him camp alone by himself and rest and pray. Rather than have him break his strict Spirit Law, they would let him break their strict laws about hunting together.

"They go too early," Uncida said to Burning Arrow on the warm spring day when the hunting party started out. "They have longed so for spring that they have forgotten the ways of the winds. They have forgotten that the wind that shakes the *tipis* in winter and goes back to the north home sometimes whirls about and comes running swiftly back."

And so it was. The weather turned cold again. The hunters found no game. Hoping to scout ducks and geese, the hunting party split up. Gideon Pond went with the smaller band, led by Round Wind. They left behind them three Dakota men, eleven women and children. Round Wind dared to leave that many women and children with only three warriors because all winter long there had been rumors of peace between the Ojibway and the Dakota. After all, the Great Father in Washington had been working for that peace ever since he had sent one of his soldier-chiefs to meet with the Indians at the meeting of the rivers many snows and grasses ago.

Because of the peace rumors, the little band of Dakota camping on the Mayawakan River did not break the Dakota law of hospitality when ten Ojibway warriors, led by the handsome and arrogant chief Hole-in-the-Day, suddenly appeared, offering to smoke the sacred pipe with them. The Dakota hunters ordered the women to kill two puppies and make a feast. They feasted. They smoked the sacred pipe together and all lay down together like blood brothers and sisters—fourteen Dakotas and ten Ojibways.

In the noon of the night the ten Ojibways silently rose and did a fearful and evil thing. They killed their Dakota hosts. Only one wounded woman and one wounded boy were alive when Gideon Pond and the other band of Dakota hunters returned to find the bodies of their relatives and friends cruelly butchered and mutilated.

"Why are Red Men not satisfied just to kill?" asked Gideon Pond as he helped the grimly silent men and their keening wives gather up the pieces of bodies and bury them on the prairie.

"Because," answered Round Wind, "we believe that in the Spirit Land we will be just as our bodies were when the spirit leaves them. The Ojibways did not want our people to have a happy time in the Spirit Land."

Small boy though he was when this happened, Burning Arrow never forgot the night after Round Wind and Gideon Pond came back with the remnant of that little band that had gone to trap and hunt on the upper Mayawakan River. Never before had he heard such heart-piercing wailing as he heard that night. It became a great chorus of grief that kept on all night long. Men and women loosened their hair, their long black hair, their pride and joy, and hacked it off with their knives. Men blackened their faces with coals from the cooking fires. Women ripped their clothes and cut off the fringes on their short gowns. Some women gashed their arms and legs until they were covered with blood.

Long past the noon of night, Burning Arrow crept into his grandmother's *tipi*, where Uncida lay on her bed, moaning softly, for her voice and her tears were gone.

"Uncida," whispered Burning Arrow, "Do not cry, I will grow big. I will grow strong. I will kill many Ojibways. I will bring you many scalps."

7

Ask the Deepest Place in Your Heart

The loud wailing of grief soon gave way to the loud chanting and drumming of war songs.

Hi! Hi! Hi!
Hi-ah-ee-ah!
Go we now!
Go we now!
Go in anger!
Go in anger!
Scalps to get!
Scalps to get!

It was Eagle Help who plotted and organized the war party that was to go into Ojibway territory and seek revenge for the treacherous killing of the three Dakota families. Burning Arrow's father did not try to hide his satisfaction in seeing the mission school's best scholar, who could now read and write the Dakota language, going against the white missionaries' teaching. Strong Heart had not liked the growing friendship between Eagle Help and Dr. Williamson, both of whom knew the healing power of roots and herbs. He was glad that the white doctor was gone for a time from the mission. He had gone back, Red Beaver said, to get the story of the son-of-god coming down to earth printed in the Dakota language on talking leaves.

Yes, they had high respect for each other, the Dakota doctor and the white doctor, but now the white grass-roots man was

45

gone and the red grass-roots man was making *wakan* and bringing himself into communion with the spirits of the dead, who would tell him in a dream or a vision where to find the enemy. At least, the spirits of the dead had always done so before!

Eagle Help made his Circle Dance, and the whole village danced with him—except Silver Woman, his own wife, who along with Hapanna and a few other women had joined the mission church and had renounced all such things.

Eagle Help dreamed his dream. Sure of victory because the spirits had promised it to him, he gathered his war party. Thirty young warriors painted themselves for going on the warpath. Thirty brave warriors fasted and prayed the Great Spirit to bless their weapons and bring them glory in battle. Some chose not to go, for that was their Dakota right. Nevertheless, those who did choose to go threw scornful words at them. "You are old women! You would rather sit home and eat sugar and wild rice than avenge braves! Why don't you wear your wife's dress and give her your breechclout?"

Red Beaver was not one of the party, for he was one of Renville's soldier-guards who lived in Tokandati. Renville wished the ancient warfare between the Dakota and the Ojibway to stop and did not wish his soldier-guards to go in Eagle Help's war party.

Strong Heart, however, painted his body for the warpath. His anger at the Ojibway for this treacherous act burned in him like a prairie fire in dry grass. Burning Arrow watched his father prepare his gun, arrows, battle axe, and knife. He and his friends tagged along behind Eagle Help, Strong Heart, and the other warriors when they went to the Mission Lodge to ask Farmer Huggins to grind enough corn to carry on this journey into enemy country. If they wished to take the enemy by surprise, they could not shoot off their guns and betray their presence.

Farmer Huggins and the new missionary, Stephen Riggs, listened gravely to the request.

"Do I understand you rightly?" asked the new missionary. "You wish us to grind corn for you to take on your war party to kill Ojibways?" Missionary Riggs placed his hand on Eagle Help's naked, painted shoulder. "Eagle Help, I am sad to see you leading this war party. You are our best scholar. You have read with your own eyes what we have written into the Dakota language. You have read that the Great God does not want his children to kill. You are asking us to help you to kill."

"If it is a killing party you are going on, I cannot grind corn for you," said Farmer Huggins.

Eagle Help shook the missionary's hand off his shoulder. His black eyes flashed with anger. "You Long Knives have the Sacred Book and know everything. Yet you Long Knives are always making war."

"What you say is true," said Missionary Riggs. "But it makes the Great God's heart sad to see men—be they white or red—kill each other."

"It is not so with the Great Spirit of the Dakota," said Strong Heart, stepping to Eagle Help's side. "He put us here on our Mother Earth expecting us to avenge wrong done to our tribe. A Dakota dishonors the Great Spirit and dishonors the dead if he does not avenge the Dakota men, women, and children the enemy kill."

"Strong Heart," said Missionary Riggs sternly, "you have a son. Would you like to see your son killed in what is nothing more than an unbroken game of revenge?"

"My son is here. Ask him what makes a Dakota father's heart glad," Strong Heart replied.

"What is your name?" asked Missionary Riggs.

Burning Arrow did not answer. A name was a private and sacred thing. It was rude of the white man to ask him his name.

"You are Sarah's son and Julia's brother?" the missionary asked.

Burning Arrow remained silent, fighting back the angry words, "I am son and brother to no one with such names."

"My son," said Strong Heart, "you do right not to answer what the missionary does not really want to know. Tell him what he really wants to know. What does a Dakota boy think in his heart about going on the warpath?"

Without hesitating, Burning Arrow answered clearly. "A Dakota brave makes himself glory if he goes on the warpath. If he kills an enemy, he makes himself gladness. If the enemy kills him,

47

the enemy makes himself glory. To kill in battle is gladness. To die in battle is glory."

"*Hau! Hau! Hau!*" shouted Eagle Help's warriors.

"All we can say," said Missionary Riggs, "is that we cannot help you. If you go on this warpath we will pray that you get no scalps."

"*Hun, hun, hay!*" shouted the warriors in anger—and turned to leave.

That night two of the mission's cows were killed, and Eagle Help's warriors feasted on beef. Soon after, they went on the warpath and crossed the imaginary line that had been set to divide the Dakotas from the Ojibways. For a month they wandered around Leech Lake but found no enemy. When they finally returned to the village—hungry, tired, frustrated, and with no scalps to stretch on hoops, no victory to sing and to drum and to dance—they killed a mission bull. To Burning Arrow's shame and disgust, his mother took Winona with her to the mission to tell the white people how bad she felt inside.

"My sister, why did she have to do that?" sputtered Burning Arrow. "Why did our mother have to go and tell the missionaries that her heart was sad about the bull? After all, it is all their fault that the war party came home without a scalp. They prayed against Eagle Help's *wakan* power!"

"And their *wakan* power was stronger than Eagle Help's *wakan* power!" said Winona. She could not keep a note of gloating out of her voice. Neither could she stop herself from teasing. "My brother, do you know what Mary Riggs said to our mother? She said she would rather have us dance around the scalp of a bull than around the scalp of an Ojibway."

"*Hanto ho!* Out of the way!" cried Burning Arrow, rushing past Winona and racing to the company of cousins whose hearts were not spoiled by white men's thoughts.

But Burning Arrow did not go at once to his playmates. Instead he went to find Uncida. Just as he expected, she was hoeing the corn plants. Just as he expected, she looked as if the corn plants were doing her a good thing instead of the other way around.

"Uncida," he asked when they were sitting under the same

cottonwood as before and had become as silent as a spider spinning the web. "Uncida, is it bad to kill the enemy?"

Uncida was silent so long that Burning Arrow wondered if she had fallen asleep. "My grandson," she said at last. "I will not hide what is in my heart. When you tell me that you will grow big and strong and bring me many enemy scalps, I tell you that you make me proud. I speak the truth. I do not lie. But I keep back something. There is a shadow in my heart. Every time our warriors come back with enemy scalps, there is a shadow in my heart."

After another long silence Uncida continued. "Tunkasida, your grandfather, once told me that he never killed a bird or an animal without feeling bad inside and asking their forgiveness. When the Dakota cut a cottonwood for the sacred sun dance pole, they apologize to the birds for taking their home. I think Wakantanka puts that shadow in our hearts whenever we kill any of his children."

"Even when we kill the enemy?"

"Even when we kill the enemy! Maybe it is because he feels a shadow in his own heart whenever one of his creatures dies."

"But my father says that Wakantanka wants Dakota men to avenge Dakota blood that is shed by the enemy," protested Burning Arrow.

"My grandson," said Uncida, "I have told you the story of the giving of the sacred pipe, the Dakota's most sacred possession."

"It was the White Buffalo Woman who brought it to the great-great-great grandfathers," said Burning Arrow, eager to show Uncida that he remembered her stories.

"After White Buffalo Woman showed our great-great-great grandfathers how to use the sacred pipe, she told them that the pipe links us to all nations on Mother Earth, to all creatures. *All,* my grandson! That is why we end our prayers and ceremonies with '*Mitakuya Owasin.*' All are my relatives. All the four-leggeds, all the two-leggeds."

"Even the enemy?" whispered Burning Arrow.

"Even the enemy, my grandson. The sacred pipe is a peacemaker. It is made from blood that has turned to stone in a place that is sacred to all nations. *All* nations, my grandson!"

49

"Even the Ojibway?" whispered Burning Arrow.

"Even the Ojibway. The red pipestone place turns even Ojibway into friends and relatives."

Burning Arrow's heart shrank and lay small upon the earth. "My heart cannot believe that," he whispered miserably. "You do not lie, my grandmother, but perhaps some grandfather many snows and grasses ago told a lie-story."

"My grandson, ask the deepest place in your heart," said Uncida. "It has the truest answer."

8

A New Name

The first wave of antimissionary feeling ebbed. Burning Arrow gradually adopted the attitude of most of the Wahpetonwan males to his mother and sister and the other Dakota women and child-women who went to worship at the mission lodge on the day the white men called holy day: "After all, it's just women who go there. No full-blooded Dakota man goes there!"

Nevertheless Burning Arrow and his friends found it hard to be indifferent to what went on at the mission lodge a half-mile away. Burning Arrow passed on to his friends every nut of news Winona brought back to their *tipi*. Winona had very quickly assumed her role of crier to his ears of all the news she heard there.

"My brother, Dr. Williamson is back!" she told him excitedly one day. "He has a new woman-child named Nancy Jane, and he brought a new teacher-woman named Fanny Huggins."

The new teacher-woman began at once to teach the Dakota women to spin and to weave. Her brother, Farmer Huggins, had a loom all made and ready for her coming. Hapanna was the one who learned to weave best. Her first creation was a white blanket spun and woven from the wool clipped from Joseph Renville's sheep. From her second piece of fabric she made a short gown for Winona. They wore their fine clothes on the holy day, and on other days they stored them away in buffalo skin parfleches in back of the beds on the woman-side of the *tipi*.

Burning Arrow still slept on the woman-side of the *tipi*, but before the first snows came he knew that his bed would quietly be moved to the man-side. He also knew that his sister-tie would soon be broken and that he could no longer look at or speak to her directly. If he wanted to tell her something, he would have to tell it to Uncida or to his mother or to his father or uncle-fathers in her hearing. If none of these people were present, then he would have to tell it to his pet wolf cub—or think out loud.

But before that direct sister-tie was broken, Winona came back one holy day with news that deeply shocked Burning Arrow, Strong Heart, Red Beaver, and every male Dakota in the Wahpetonwan village on the Lac qui Parle. A full-blooded Dakota man had brought shame to every man and boy in the village! A full-blooded Dakota man had had the saving waters poured on his head and allowed himself to be called Simon. Winona's report proved to be true. A full-blooded Dakota man had indeed gone over to the white man's way. All the way! He put away the breechclout and blanket he wore for every day, the vest, leggings, and headdress he wore for feasts and dances, *and put on white men's clothing.* He stopped using his naked body as a skin on which to paint Indian meanings. He let the missionaries cut off his long black hair, the badge of Dakota manhood. Indeed, he looked so ridiculous with his hair sticking up like porcupine quills that the first time his wife saw him that way she burst into loud wails and rushed into her *tipi.* Moreover, he planted a field of corn and potatoes next to the mission garden and hoed in it like any woman. Worse yet, he began helping the missionaries and the Dakota Christian women make sun-burnt bricks for the *tipiwakan,* the church they were building into the hillside above the Lac qui Parle.

And who was this defector from the Good Red Road? It was Aniwegamani, the Dakota warrior who in battles with the Ojibway had done more daring deeds than any other warrior. No one of them had killed more enemy and counted more coups than he!

"My father, why don't the *akicita*-police punish him and kill his dog and break his gun and cut his blanket and slash his *tipi?*" Burning Arrow asked his father.

"Because it is Aniwegamani," Strong Heart answered.

52

Burning Arrow now learned for the first time that no Dakota, not even an *akicita*, dared punish another Dakota who had done greater deeds and shown himself braver than he. A Dakota man ranks above anyone who has not done as brave deeds as he has done. Indeed, a Dakota woman who has done a great and brave deed ranks above any Dakota man who has not done as great and brave a deed. In a way, such a Dakota man or woman is above the law.

But Aniwegamani was not above being laughed at and screamed at by Burning Arrow and all his playmates, with the exception of Jean Baptiste. All but Jean Baptiste followed Aniwegamani to his garden and hurled scorn words at him. "Look at the man who makes himself into a woman!"

When Burning Arrow and his friends found out that the name the missionaries had given Aniwegamani was Simon, they ran around his wife's *tipi* shouting at the top of their lungs. "Simon Cut Hair! Simon Cut Hair! Where are you?"

Other children joined the whirling dance, laughing and shouting. The village dogs ran in and out between their legs, barking.

Suddenly above the din Burning Arrow heard his name called. It was Red Beaver, his uncle-father, coming from Tokandati the Soldier Lodge. Something in Red Beaver's face told Burning Arrow what to expect—a stern scolding. Whenever he needed a severe scolding, it was Red Beaver who gave it to him—not Strong Heart, his father, or Hapanna, his mother. Dakota fathers and mothers were not for scolding. Dakota fathers and mothers were for loving.

Burning Arrow followed Red Beaver to the top of the hill from which one could look across the Lac qui Parle to the prairie country stretching to where the sky rubbed against Mother Earth. Red Beaver stood so still and so long still facing the setting sun that he could have been a sunpole tree. Burning Arrow stood just as straight and tall as he was tall, but inside he felt crooked and small.

At last Red Beaver spoke. "My nephew, who are you?"

"My uncle, I am a Dakota."

"My nephew, you are a boy-man and not too young to hear truths. Open your ears and hear what I say. Four is a sacred number for the Dakota nation. Before a Dakota man smoke-prays he holds his sacred pipe silently to the four winds. When he smokes in council meetings, he takes four puffs before he passes the pipe to another. The body has four faces—front, back, left, right. There are four true colors—black, red, yellow, white. There are four women-virtues—bravery, generosity, thankfulness, bearing children. There are four man-virtues—bravery, generosity, endurance, and wisdom. A Dakota honors bravery, generosity, endurance, and wisdom in others. No Dakota warrior of our band has been more brave and generous than Aniwegamani. No brave has suffered more in silence than he."

Burning Arrow's eyes flashed. "Those are only *three* virtues! You left out one—wisdom. Can you say that Aniwegamani is wise and speak the truth, my father-uncle?"

Red Beaver looked at the sky where the sun was painting long ribbons in the most sacred color of all. In a voice so soft that Burning Arrow could barely hear it, he said, "Only someone who is as wise as Wakantanka can say if Aniwegamani is wise. Are you that wise?"

The second wave of antimissionary feeling was stronger and more violent than the first one and this time was directed against the Christian Dakota as well as the missionaries. Perhaps the resentment was stronger this time because the Wahpetonwan Dakota on the Lac qui Parle found so many reasons for it and heard so many rumors to sluice into it. For example, frost blackened the young corn and killed all the flowers that bore fruit, the fruit in flower. The women planted the last remaining corn, but wind galloped over the land and brought no rain. The lakes and ponds shriveled and shrank, and the muskrats grew scarcer than scarce. What did it all mean but that Wakantanka had turned his back on his Dakota children? What had changed his heart? It was the presence of the missionaries, of course! Wakantanka was angry because some of his Dakota children were leaving the Good Red Road!

The rumors that fed the antimissionary feeling came from the Dakota bands near the meeting of the two great rivers. The winters since those Mdewakantonwan bands had sold to the

54

white men their claim to all the lands east of the Mississippi and the islands therein numbered the fingers on one hand. Yet not a penny of the $5000 a year they had been told the Great Father in Washington would give them for the education of their children had come. Why?

"Because the missionaries are getting the money," some of the fur traders who hated the influence of the missionaries slyly told them. "Take your children out of their schools. Have nothing to do with the missionaries."

When their demands for the education money continued to be ignored, the Eastern bands of the Dakota began to think that the thriving mission school at Lac qui Parle was to blame. They instigated the Wahpetonwan Dakota to take their children out of school, to harass the missionaries and the Christian Indians, and to kill the mission cattle. The *akicita*-police now stationed themselves along the path to the adobe church and school and turned back the children. Hearing of their plans to cut the blankets of those who went to worship in the church on the holy day, Burning Arrow said to his mother, "Someone should not wear the beautiful white blanket today."

But the Wahpetonwan Dakota could hardly blame the missionaries for the whiskey that began to be brought into the village from the new white man's town rapidly growing on the east bank of the Mississippi on the land the Eastern bands had just sold to the white man. But the missionaries were *white* men, after all, and the new evil came from the *white* men. White men were responsible for the poison that made fools of Dakota men.

"When a Dakota man gives poison he kills one man," said Strong Heart bitterly after a drunken orgy in the village in which two men were killed. "The white man's poison kills a man and his family and friends as well."

So it was in the hope of turning Wakantanka's face around to his Dakota children again that an expedition of about 20 of the principal men of the village went to the sacred pipestone quarries in that bad summer. Strong Heart and his brother Red Beaver were among them. The kind fur trader Joseph Renville lent them his horses and new wagons with the iron-banded wheels in which to carry back the sacred stone from which to make the pipes that were the Dakota sacred symbol of truth. Burning Arrow and his friends followed the wagons until Strong Heart sent them back.

"My son," he said, "perhaps on the way back we will shoot an antelope or a deer and we can at last give the Naming Feast for you."

But there was no returning to the village on the Lac qui Parle for Strong Heart, for Wakinyan, the winged thunder being who hurls the *wakan* fire, struck him down two sleeps away. The too-late rains came in a dreadful storm, and the fire that flashes and burns like blue flames found the men crouching for shelter under the wagons with the iron-banded wheels. When Wakinyan, the thunder being, had flown away, three men and two horses were dead and Strong Heart and Eagle Help were badly burned. Red Beaver and those whom the thunder being had not touched buried the dead, tenderly lay the silently suffering burned ones in the carts with the iron-banded wheels, and turned back to the village. But Strong Heart was burned over so much of his body that he knew that he was dying. Because the jolting of the wagon added to his suffering, Red Beaver and the others stopped the horses under a clump of cottonwoods.

"My brother," said Strong Heart weakly but bitterly, "it does not matter where you bury me. Wherever it is, the white man's roads will pass over my grave. My grave will be a white farmer's field, and my bones will be plowed up."

Strong Heart's last breath spoke Burning Arrow's new name. Red Beaver had to lean close to his mouth to hear it. "My . . . son . . . shall be called . . . One Loon."

56

9

They Carry But Little

So the wagons with the iron-banded wheels returned to the village on the Lac qui Parle carrying not loads of sacred red stone for the sacred pipes, but Dakota warriors painfully burned by the man-killing mystery that lives in the clouds. When they arrived, the village was already loud with grief, for Red Beaver had run ahead carrying in his heart the heavy load of the deaths. The grief was hardest to bear for the wives of the men buried on the prairie, for they could do nothing to help their husbands' spirits break their earth bonds and move easily along the last spirit trail. They could not wash their bodies, rub them with sacred red paint, and wrap them in their finest blankets. They could not lay their bodies on burial platforms on the ridge over-looking the Lac qui Parle until the flesh had left the bones. They could not reverently make a bundle of the bones and bury them in a sacred place.

But the hardest grief belonged to Hapanna, for she loved Strong Heart as much now as she had loved him when he had played the flute all night long outside her mother's *tipi* at Kaposia. She knew, too, that he had never ceased to love her, for he had never taken another wife. Some of the Dakota men had taken three. For example, the son of the old chieftain Little Crow at Kaposia had come to live with the Wahpetonwan band and had married three daughters of their chief.

"Jesus, have mercy on his soul!" shrieked Hapanna when Red Beaver brought the sad news to her *tipi*. She was sure that

Strong Heart's soul would forever be in the place for souls that had not had the Saving Waters and did not believe in the Great God and the Son of God. But even though she had decided to follow the Jesus road all the way, she expressed her grief in all the traditional Dakota ways.

"Wakantanka, have mercy on us!" moaned Uncida, who was sure that Strong Heart's spirit was on the way to the campfire of good Dakota spirits but was also quite sure that his death was a punishment for her daughter's leaving the Good Red Road.

"Ate! Ate!" wailed Burning Arrow and Winona, sure of nothing but that they would never see their beloved father again.

Several days later Red Beaver took Burning Arrow to the hill overlooking Lac qui Parle and told him his father's last word, the father-child-name by which he would now be called: One Loon.

Reading Burning Arrow's thinking question in his eyes, Red Beaver answered it quietly. "My nephew, because the spirit of my brother, your father, saw a brother in the loon's spirit." Something within him asked him not to tell his young nephew that Strong Heart's far-seeing eyes had seen loneliness and sadness ahead for his son and all the Dakota. His dying eyes had seen the loneliness and sadness the loon cries hauntingly on its northward flight to lonely lakes.

Because a Dakota never says his or her own name, Red Beaver announced to Uncida, Hapanna, and Winona what Strong Heart's mouth spoke before his spirit left his body. Thus it was that there was no Naming Feast for One Loon but only the ceremony of Give-Away. Whenever a close relative's spirit has gone on the road of spirits, his closest of kin give to the needy. Some give away until they have nothing left but their sorrow and the clothes on their backs. The more they give away, the more honor they do to the departed spirit. Nothing is too precious to give in the Give-Away ceremony. Hapanna gave her fine woven blanket to an old Wahpetonwan woman as blind and helpless as a newborn pup. When One Loon saw that the lines on the old woman's face were like many dry stream beds leading to the deep dry hollows of her cheeks, he gave the most precious thing he had. With his own hands he carried a wooden bowl of soup made from his own pet, his tamed wolf cub, to the old woman. If only he were old enough and strong enough to kill a fat bear and give a feast for all the hungry in the village, for there were so many, so many! In every *tipi* there was the dark shadow of famine.

After the *akicita* roughly prevented Hapanna and Winona and the other Christian Dakota women from going to the adobe church on the next holy day and told them that they were to blame for Strong Heart's death, Hapanna suddenly decided to take her little family back to Kaposia where she had been born and where Strong Heart had wooed and won her at a big summer meeting of the four Eastern bands of the Dakota nation. Uncida was so happy over the decision that she softly crooned a song.

> I wish to die
> where I was born,
> where I was born.
> I wish to die
> where I first loved,
> where I first loved.
> It is the most beautiful land
> on our Mother Earth.
> It is the center,
> it is the heart,
> of our Mother the Earth.

"My grandmother, is Kaposia really the center of Mother Earth?" asked One Loon in surprise. He knew that Uncida, like Marguerite, the late wife of Joseph Renville, was a Dakota of the Mdewakantonwan tribe and had been born at Kaposia. He knew, too, that Tunkasida was buried there. But that Kaposia was the *center* of Mother Earth!

"The place where the Minnesota flows into the Mississippi is right over the center of Mother Earth," said Uncida firmly.

"Is that why the Mdewakantonwan are so proud and think

59

that they are the most important tribe in the world?" asked One Loon.

"And so we are, my grandson!" exclaimed Uncida.

Now the tears that streaked One Loon's charcoal-painted face were not just tears for his father. One Loon, the man-boy, knew that a Dakota male could cry at the death of relatives but should not cry about moving away from dear familiar faces and places. Nevertheless, for a brief time One Loon, the man-boy, was Burning Arrow, the boy-man, again and cried in secret at the thought of moving away from Red Beaver, his uncle-father, and all the relatives and *hunka*-relatives. Far, far from his friends, especially Jean Baptiste. Far, far from the Lac qui Parle, its boulders and islands, the finest playground a Dakota boy could have.

Play? Would he ever play again? The crow-birds of mischief had swooped down into his life, his inside life as well as his outside life. Would he ever again feel like making a song, an inside song? Would he ever again feel as if the Great Mystery, Wakantanka, looked down on him with love?

"Wakantanka, Great Mystery," prayed Burning Arrow, the boy-man. "I have been a little boy long enough. Help me to be a brave Dakota man. Help me to be strong. Help me to walk in my father's moccasins."

One Loon, the man-boy, stood up and wiped the tears from his face.

Young as he was, One Loon saw and wondered at Red Beaver's face when his mother told him that the four of them were going to start at once for Kaposia. Young as he was, he could see that his uncle-father was struggling to make his face a no-telling face.

"Stay!" Red Beaver exclaimed, almost harshly.

"For what is there to stay?" asked Hapanna tonelessly. "My husband has gone to the land of spirits. Dr. Williamson and his family have gone from the mission."

"Only for a few moons," said Red Beaver. "Williamson went away once before and came back. He will come back again."

But nothing Red Beaver said could change Hapanna's heart. Neither could her Jesus-sisters.

"Wait!" they pleaded. "Wait, and we will go, too. If the *akicita* will not let our children go to the mission school or go to worship on the Holy Day, we will go with you to Kaposia."

But Hapanna would neither stay nor wait. Before dawn one morning she swiftly and quietly took down Uncida's *tipi* (she had given her own away in the Give-Away ceremony), and the four of them stole away toward the dawn-rosy sky. The few belongings they had left were not too much for the grandmother, mother, and daughter backs.

Uncida softly sang a song as they walked:

> We carry but little.
> We carry but little.
> Only our sorrow.
> Only our spirits.
> Sorrow rides heavily.
> A good spirit rides lightly.

Hapanna and Winona recited something they had learned at the mission:

> *Wonmakiye cin Jehowa hee:*
> *Takudan imakakije kte sni.*
> *Peji toto en iwanke maye kta;*
> *Wicoozi mini kin icahda yus amaye kta.*

> (The Lord is my shepherd,
> I shall not want;
> he makes me lie down
> in green pastures.
> He leads me beside still waters.)

One Loon sang nothing and said nothing. He walked ahead of the three women, carrying his bow and arrow and turning his head to all the directions, watching for the enemy.

They had walked about five miles on the worn ox-cart trail and were just about to cross the Mayawakan River when Red Beaver overtook them. He was riding one of Renville's horses and leading a spotted pony saddled with parfleches and pulling

61

a pony-drag. Silently he handed the lead reins of the spotted pony to Hapanna, turned his horse, and galloped back to the village in a cloud of dust.

"My husband's brother could not let his brother's family come to Kaposia like beggars," said Hapanna as she packed Uncida's *tipi* and the bundle Uncida had been carrying on the pony drag.

Uncida, however, had other thoughts. She knew why Red Beaver had never taken a wife. She knew how long Red Beaver had hidden his love for Hapanna in his heart. She knew that it was too soon for him to speak his heart to her. She knew why Hapanna had received this gift of a spotted pony and parfleches filled with jerky meat for the long journey to Kaposia.

The spotted pony drove many of the shadows out of One Loon's heart and became to him like a *hunka*-brother. No longer did he awake at night and think only of how it was before his father went away. Now he lay thinking of what he and Spotted Pony could do to bring his little thistledown wisp of a grandmother safely to Kaposia. *Uncida stumbled today,* he thought to himself. *Tomorrow she must ride the pony drag.*

But it took something else to bring back a smile to Hapanna's face again. That same "something else" made a small shadow in One Loon's heart bigger and darker! Guarding his eyes carefully as was proper for a man-son with his mother, One Loon watched her as she made their night camps on the prairie. There was nothing wrong with the soup she cooked in the iron kettle from a piece of jerky and drought-shriveled wild turnips she had dug along the trail, but there was everything wrong with her hacked uncombed hair, her gloomy unwashed face, and her weary, stooped shoulders. Even when they camped at Shakopee's village and Good Road's village, she did not wash her face or comb her hair.

But what a change came over her when she learned at Black Dog's village that Dr. Williamson and his family were staying nearby with Gideon Pond's family! As soon as she and Winona had bathed in the river and combed their hair, they grabbed the lead reins of the spotted pony and ran with the fleetest of feet to the missionary's cabin. Uncida bounced along behind on the pony drag, followed by One Loon.

One Loon could not believe his eyes and his ears when he saw how the white missionary families greeted his mother and sister. "Sarah! Julia! Is it really you?"

Over and over again! The laughter! The hand-touching and handshaking the men and boys did. The hugging and kissing the women did! As if Hapanna and Winona were their true sisters. As true sisters as were Pond's woman and Williamson's woman! As if his mother and sister were white women and not full-blooded Dakota women!

One Loon was equally amazed at the missionaries' tears when his mother told them about the killing and wounding of the Dakotas by the mysterious fire from the clouds. Tears were the water of blood-relatives and *hunka*-relatives! White people could *never* be relatives—no more than day could be night or night day. Wakantanka had made it so!

One Loon and Uncida politely refused the missionaries' invitation to eat the evening meal with them. While Uncida set up her tent an arrow's flight from Gideon Pond's cabin, One Loon took Spotted Pony to the river to drink. It was the same river as the river that made the Lac qui Parle, but here at the ending of its waters its spirit did not seem to speak to his spirit. Neither did the spirits of the trees here. Where had all the good spirits fled?

For one brief moment One Loon saw a friendly good spirit peering through the eyes of young John Williamson when the boy brought two bowls of steaming potatoes and turnips to the *tipi* for Uncida and himself. But One Loon's black eyes swiftly slid away and refused to greet the good spirit looking at him from his old playmate's eyes. For Uncida's sake he accepted the food and thanked John politely.

Later, wrapped in his blanket outside the door of Uncida's *tipi,* he listened to the singing in Pond's log lodge. His mother and Winona were still there, singing Jesus songs along with the missionaries.

"Uncida, my grandmother," One Loon called softly, "my heart

tells me that my mother and my sister have left the Good Red Road forever!"

Uncida did not speak, but he heard her weeping softly.

"*Ate! Ate!* Father, Father! I wish you were here!" One Loon murmured. But since that could not be, One Loon fell asleep praying a wish-prayer: "My uncle-father, we need you! My uncle-father, come soon!"

10

Kaposia

Red Beaver did come to Kaposia, but not until as many moons had born and died as the fingers on One Loon's two hands and the toes on one foot. And not until One Loon had sadly learned that in Kaposia the Dakota way was fast becoming no good. True, the Mdewakantonwan band on the west bank of the Mississippi below the meeting of the waters of the two rivers had not given up all the old Dakota ways. They had not given up smoking the sacred pipe, the sweat bath, the favorite Dakota sport—lacrosse, the Give-Away ceremony, the traditional feasts and dances, painting their bodies, going on the warpath against the Ojibway, counting coup, and taking scalps. In the Wild Rice Drying Moon, when Hapanna brought her family to Kaposia, the band was still dancing with the Ojibway scalps they had taken on the St. Croix in an avenging party for the three of their band who had been surprised by Ojibways and killed and scalped. From Uncida's relatives, in whose bark summer lodge they stayed as guests for a time, One Loon heard over and over again the stories of the attack avenging the Dakota victims.

The night sounds in Kaposia were the same night sounds One Loon had known in the village on the Lac qui Parle: the plaintive music of flutes played by lovelorn Dakota braves outside the *tipis* or bark lodges of the beloved, the chanting of a medicine man trying to drive some bad spirit from a sick person, the thumming and drumming of initiates dancing outside a warrior

65

lodge, the low voice of an old warrior telling stories of Dakota bravery to young ears.

But there were night sounds in Kaposia that were new to One Loon's ears—sounds that send him scurrying back to Uncida's *tipi* where he pulled the covers over his head and fiercely wished that they had never left the Wahpetonwan village so many sleeps away. They were the sounds of drunken orgies when the Kaposian men gathered around a keg of whiskey that someone had bought from a white man across the river and paid for with a horse or blankets or traps or furs—anything for the white man's poison fire that made Indians feel big and bold but took away all their senses and dignity. On such nights blood and *hunka* bonds, man and wife bonds, father and children bonds meant nothing. Dakota men knifed each other, broke each other's ribs, and bit off each other's noses. Dakota husbands beat their wives and children. Strong and sturdy Dakota men fell into cooking fires and burned or fell into the river and drowned. They shot off guns wildly and sometimes shot each other. On such nights the women of Kaposia wore their moccasins to bed and were prepared to flee with their children to the hills above the village. If the drunken orgy lasted several days, they hid their husbands' guns—until the day a small Ojibway party sneaked into the cornfield and scalped some women hoeing corn and the aroused Kaposian men could not find their guns.

One early evening One Loon saw a drunken company of Kaposian men scattered before it could become an orgy—and by a woman! Brandishing a battle axe, Eyatonkawin, a Wahpekute woman married to a Mdewakantonwan warrior, marched into the center of their circle, placed a foot on the keg of whiskey, and eloquently recited the brave deed she had once done. Surprised by a band of Sac Indians from the south, her first husband, a Wahpekute brave, had been killed before her eyes at the door of her *tipi*. Laying down her newborn baby, she had seized her husband's war axe and killed three enemy one by one as they stepped over her husband's body and stooped to enter her *tipi*.

"Not one of you has done a braver deed than that!" shouted

66

Eyatonkawin, and proceeded to smash the keg of whiskey. And not one Kaposian male dared to raise a hand or a voice against this woman, for what she said was true! Not one of them had done a braver deed than her brave deed.

It was another strong-heart woman who explained when and why and how the whiskey craze and the brawls had started. She was called She Gathers Huckleberries and she was Uncida's childhood and girlhood friend. Meeting her again had brought the light back to Uncida's eyes and laughter to her lips. Meeting her for the first time made One Loon secretly choose her for his *hunka*-grandmother.

"Open your ears when my sister-friend She Gathers Huckleberries speaks," Uncida told Winona and One Loon. "What she knows is worth knowing."

"It all began so many years ago," explained She Gathers Huckleberries, holding up all five gnarled fingers of one of her scarred hands. "It began when we Mdewakantonwans agreed to give the Great Father in Washington the land east of the Mississippi and the Great Father in Washington agreed to give us money and food and schools for our children. But the schools never did come, and the white men who came to live on the land came with whiskey. That is how it all began."

"My sister," said Uncida quietly, "how can we Mdewakantonwans give something we do not own? The land belongs to Mother Earth."

"It makes no difference to the white men if the land belongs to Mother Earth," answered She Gathers Huckleberries grimly. "If they want it, they take it."

"If the white men cross the Mississippi, we will make war on them!" said One Loon fiercely.

She Gathers Huckleberries sighed heavily. "Our old warriors with eagle hearts are dying. Our young warriors have rabbit hearts. Some of them do not even hunt any more. They just squat and smoke and talk big words and wait for money. When they get it, they buy horses and whiskey, and the whiskey makes them fools."

On the white man's Holy Day Winona and Hapanna rose quietly and slipped away before dawn to walk to Gideon Pond's mission lodge to sing Dakota hymns and worship the great God and Son of God with the missionary families and a small group of Dakota who were walking the Jesus road. On such days the two old grandmother friends did their work and then sat talking about how the old ways were changing. One Loon, who had not found a *hunka*-friend yet and felt lonely and alone, often sat and listened to them.

"Haaay! Haaay!" sighed She Gathers Huckleberries. "Children are not as polite now as we were when we were children. We never entered a closed *tipi* unless we were invited. Now they just walk in. They even walk between the fire and guests. Nor do they eat everything that is served them. What is the world coming to!"

"My grandson," asked Uncida, "is it true that some young boys smoke the sacred pipe before they have sought a vision and before they have done a manly deed?"

"It has happened," answered One Loon, wondering guiltily if Uncida knew that he had already done so with Jean Baptiste and his friends back at Lac qui Parle.

"But saddest of all here at Kaposia is that people do not live in the sacred way as they used to. They do not fast and pray. The men in Kaposia seem to care only for themselves. They do not feel for their wives and children and friends. They do not care for their great Dakota nation."

"I saw it coming in our village on the Lac qui Parle," murmured Uncida.

The two old grandmothers fell into a long silence. One Loon felt as if they had climbed a hill so high that rivers looked like ribbons and were looking down at the ways of man.

"Tell me, my sister," said Uncida at last, "have they danced the Sun Dance at Kaposia since that day when—?"

"That day when Rides Buffalo, your husband, danced it? That time when our village was across the river at the *wakan* Red Rock?"

"Do you mean Tunkasida, my grandfather?" asked One Loon eagerly. Uncida had told him about the time Tunkasida had saved himself from being trampled under the buffalo herd by leaping onto a young bull's back. But never had she told him that Tunkasida had danced the Sun Dance, the most sacred of all the Dakota dances, the dance that no Dakota could do for the sake of pride or praise, for pain danced with him from sun-up until sun-down. The dance that no Dakota did for his own sake but only for the sake of his people.

"When the white soldiers and their chief came to build a fort near our village at the *wakan* Red Rock," said Uncida, "many in our village saw a black road of difficulties ahead for the Dakota nation. Our head men decided that our strongest and bravest young warriors should dance the Sun Dance and bring *wakan* power back to our people for the hard time ahead. Your grandfather was one of the young men invited to dance the sacred dance, and it was he who danced the longest. For four days, when the sun was at its strongest, he danced. He danced until the rawhide thongs that led from the top of the Holy Tree to the pierced flesh of his breasts broke the flesh and he fell into a vision sleep."

"My grandmother, was he hurt?" whispered One Loon. "Was my grandfather hurt?"

"Your grandfather was full of *wakan* power and could not be hurt," said Uncida. "But he was scarred. I am sure that the Ojibway who took his scalp saw the Sun Dance scars and knew that he had killed a good and a great enemy of his people."

"And now," Uncida said bitterly after a long silence, "and now your grandfather's bones are becoming dust in the land across the river that the white men think they own."

"And my father's bones are becoming dust somewhere on the wide prairie!" cried One Loon. "And there is no one to bring food offerings to his spirit as it takes its last farewell to his body!"

In a rage of loneliness and despair One Loon rushed out of the *tipi*. Seeing the young lads of the village running races on the river bank, he turned to climb the high ridge above the river and Little Crow's village. Since he had screamed and run in terror when he had first heard and then seen what he thought was a dreadful monster belching smoke coming up the river, the Kaposian boys had thrown scorn words and scorn laughter at him.

"*Haho'! Haho'!*" they had shouted. "The Wahpetonwan boy is afraid of the fire boat!" In fact, after that they had called him Boy Afraid of Fire Boat.

At the top of the ridge One Loon could see far. To the south and east was the Red Rock prairie, where the crumbling-to-dust bones of his grandfather lay in what was now White Man's Land. Across the river in White Man's Land were the log lodges of the white whiskey traders. To the west were the lodges of the white men's fort with the white men's sacred symbol flying above it. On the south bank of the Minnesota, where it joined the Mississippi, stood the lodges of the white fur traders Sibley and Faribault. Down there, too, in Gideon Pond's mission lodge hidden in an oak grove, his mother and sister were singing and praying to the white men's god and son-of-god.

One Loon raised his eyes to the bundled body on the burial scaffold above his head. He did not know whose body it was, but for a moment he wishfully felt that it was his father's body and cried out the thought that haunted his heart night and day. "*Ate! Ate!* If the *heyoka* had been with you and the others that night and danced on moccasinned hands, would the *heyoka* have kept the thunder being from hurling his *wakan* fire at you and killing you?"

In time the Kaposian boys called One Loon by his true name, his father-name, but not until he had proved himself as tough a wrestler and as fleet of foot as the best of them—indeed, the fleetest of any and all of them. Yet One Loon's heart did not feel strong and whole and manful—not even when he had shot wild fowl with his bow and arrow or caught a fish through the ice for his mother's iron kettle. The strong-heart feeling did not return for a whole year. It came back to him after their return from the wild rice harvest. They were all resting in Uncida's *tipi* when there was a scratching at the closed flap. Winona peered out and cried out in joy. "*Hee-noo!* It is our uncle-father!"

It was Red Beaver, who had ridden alone from Lac qui Parle to take Hapanna as his wife and to be a father to Winona and

70

One Loon. Even though Red Beaver was her second true love, Hapanna was as happy as a young girl who marries her first true love. Yet she was no happier than One Loon, who suddenly felt strong and whole again.

Indeed, so happy was he that he even went along to Gideon Pond's mission lodge, where Dr. Williamson married his mother and Red Beaver in a white man's ceremony. He did not even wince when Dr. Williamson used his mother's saving water's name and called her Sarah! So happy was he that day that he had a shy smile for everybody—for the aunt-sister everyone called Aunt Jane, who had come that summer from the faraway home to help Dr. Williamson, for young John Williamson, who was carrying his little sister Nancy Jane with the bad back as if he had been born with her on his own back. When One Loon learned that the Williamsons were soon leaving to return to their mission lodge on the Lac qui Parle, he overcame his shyness enough to ask young John to talk to his brother friend, his *koda*-friend, Jean Baptiste Renville, and tell him that all was well with One Loon, who had been called Burning Arrow.

11

Whys That Buzz Like Flies

So it was Red Beaver, after he and Hapanna returned from a five-sleep journey alone to the Standing Rock River, who taught One Loon the manly arts of hunting and fishing and all the secrets of finding game, like listening to the humming of the deer flies to find out where deer is hiding. It was Red Beaver, too, who took him on two or three sleep's journeys to teach him to discipline his body and to go without food and water. On these journeys One Loon learned silence and felt its holiness.

One evening when they had gone from sunrise to sunset without speaking, Red Beaver said, "Maybe, my son, if you learn silence when you are young, you may grow a thought that will help our people."

"Maybe someday I will dance the Sun Dance for our people," said One Loon.

Red Beaver also taught One Loon how to be a warrior, and in this he was a stern teacher.

"A Dakota warrior is prepared even in sleep," he told One Loon one morning when One Loon objected to being awakened out of a sound sleep by a bloodcurdling war whoop over his head and was expected to grab a weapon and leap like a cougar to attack the attackers.

"A Dakota warrior is like an animal in the wild. Here in Kaposia the Dakotas are becoming like tame animals. A tamed animal forgets to be watchful. A Dakota warrior never ceases to watch for the enemy," said Red Beaver. He told One Loon of the surprise attack on the relatives of the two Wahpetonwan youths Missionary Riggs had taken to Ohio with him. It had happened just last summer when the watchers on the hills above the Lac qui Parle had spotted the party of returning missionaries in the distance. The relatives of the two youths had wished to meet them and in their joy forgot to watch for the enemy. A small band of Ojibways surprised them and took two scalps. The enemy rode on to meet the returning whites and greeted them as friends. The two returning Dakota youths, who looked like white men with their short hair and white men's clothes, *shook hands with the Ojibways who had just minutes before killed their relatives and carried their bloody scalps on their belts!*

One Loon told Red Beaver of the surprise attack on the Kaposian women in the cornfield while the Kaposian men lay in a drunken stupor.

"If the Ojibways had known that, they could have killed every man, woman, and child in the village!" said Red Beaver.

Whiskey, the white man's poison water, did in fact almost destroy the village of Kaposia before it was finally destroyed forever by the white men crossing the Mississippi. In the year 1845 by the white man's count the old chief Little Crow died. She Gathers Huckleberries told Uncida that she was sure that his death was hastened by losing two of his seven sons on an avenging raid into Ojibway territory. The dying chief chose his son Little Crow to be the next chief. Uncida was sure that he chose him because whiskey had already made the other sons unfit to be leaders. And Little Crow the Younger was perhaps the fittest because he had been living in the village on the Lac qui Parle, many sleeps away from the white men's whiskey village on the east side of the Mississippi.

Little Crow came back to Kaposia quickly with his three wives and children and claimed the position of chief. His jealous brothers, however, did not recognize his claim.

"My brother is not even a Mdewakantonwan or a Kaposian," One Loon heard one brother say jeeringly to a group of young men playing the card game they had learned from the whiskey traders across the river. "My brother has married Wahpetonwan women and made his crow's nest in the Wahpetonwan village."

In a drunken spree two of the brothers tried to kill Little Crow and shattered both his wrists. In the shooting spree that followed, the two brothers were killed. Little Crow was rushed to the white doctor at the soldiers' fort. When the white doctor saw the condition of Little Crow's hands and wrists, he had but one word to say: "Amputate!"

"What does he say?" Little Crow asked the interpreter.

"He says 'Cut them off!' "

"Cut them off?" roared Little Crow. "Get out!"

Little Crow was brought back to Kaposia and the Dakota medicine man was summoned. He carefully picked out the splintered small bones, applied ground-up roots, and splinted the broken bones. When one moon had come and gone and another one was beginning, Little Crow was using his hands again. Ugly, scarred, and crippled they were, to be sure, but they could grasp a gun. Hapanna, who considered Missionary-Doctor Williamson the greatest doctor in the world, agreed that even he could not have done better.

The bodies of Little Crow's two brothers were not honored by being placed on a burial platform on the hilltop but were buried at the center of the village to be trampled underfoot, even by dogs.

It was precisely the craze for whiskey in the village of Kaposia and the drunken shooting spree that shattered Little Crow's wrists that eventually brought Dr. Williamson and his family to Kaposia. While he was living on the Lac qui Parle, Little Crow's eyes and ears had not been shut to the work of the missionary families. However, it was not any interest in the white man's god and son-of-god that led him to ask the Soldier Chief at the fort to get him a missionary. It was, instead, a desperate hope that a missionary at Kaposia could wean his men from drinking the poison that was destroying them. As for Dr. Williamson, he no doubt was influenced to come by the fact that the chief of the Mdewakantonwan band at Kaposia *wanted* a missionary, whereas the leaders of the Wahpetonwan band on the Lac qui Parle were doing everything short of harming them bodily to show them that they did not want them there. Moreover, in the Moon of Snow Blindness Joseph Renville, the great and good friend and helper of the missionaries, had died.

One Loon and his whole family were gone on a long fall-into-winter hunt above and below the Standing Rock River when Dr. Williamson and his family arrived at Kaposia. For One Loon those five months away from the village were the last totally unshadowed moons in his life. The best hunters in the Mdewakantonwan villages clustered near the meeting of the waters went on the hunt and pledged themselves to keep the strict rules of life on the hunt. No whiskey drinking! No crossing the daily boundaries set by the *akicita*-police selected for the hunt. Even the chiefs and the white fur traders, if they happened to be along on the hunt, had to obey the strict laws of the hunt.

Every able-bodied member of a hunter's family went along— even Uncida! Indeed, One Loon could not remember when in all his 13 winters Uncida had been so able-bodied and cheerful. Once again she could pitch a *tipi* properly and take it down again as fast as her daughter Hapanna. Because she was so competent and happy and cheerful, the women asked her to supervise the work of preparing the hides for new *tipi* covers. Only someone who thought good thoughts was supposed to do that— otherwise the new *tipi* would smoke or go down in a high wind.

Once again One Loon heard Uncida sing songs she made up herself:

It is like the old times.
It is like the good times.
Men bringing meat.
Women skinning.
Women scraping.
Women drying.
Soup in the kettle.
Meat simmering.
Good! Good!
Everything good!

When the Mdewakantonwans returned from the hunt, they had the tanned hides of 2000 deer, 60 elk, 12 bear, ten buffalo, and six cougar—and meat enough to feed everybody until the fat full moons of summer.

When Little Crow's people returned to Kaposia, they found Missionary-Doctor Williamson living in the log lodge built ten years before by Methodist missionaries and abandoned when the mission was closed.

"The whole family!" reported Winona, who had immediately run to pay a visit. "Father and Mother Williamson, John, Andrew, Nancy Jane, Smith, and Baby Martha! Dr. Williamson's sister Aunt Jane. And—and—you cannot guess! Marguerite Renville! My friend, Marguerite! She has come along to live with the Williamsons."

"Is my friend Jean Baptiste along?" asked One Loon eagerly, forgetting for a moment that he was not supposed to talk directly to his sister.

"No," answered Winona, looking boldly and directly at him, for she insisted that there was nothing in the Great God's ten Spirit Laws that said, "Thou shalt not look at or talk directly to thy sisters after thou hast put away thy little-boy name." Neither did Jesus teach that it was wrong for sisters to talk directly with brothers, or, for that matter, for mothers-in-law and sons-in-law to look at each other and talk directly together! Winona had tried to tell that to Uncida when Uncida chose to move to She Gathers Huckleberries' *tipi* after Red Beaver had become her son-in-law, but Uncida as usual shut her ears to changing-ways talk.

"Tell someone we know that no Dakota brave will marry her if she scorns the Dakota ways," said One Loon to Red Beaver, who was cleaning his rifle. One Loon knew that Winona was ready for marriage, for every time the moon was a silver canoe in the night sky, she went to the woman-alone *tipi*.

"I shall not marry a husband unless he follows the Jesus way," said Winona pertly.

"Ask someone we know if she would marry a white man," One Loon said to Red Beaver.

"If I loved him and if he loved Jesus," answered Winona simply.

"Ask someone we know if she would marry an Ojibway," One Loon asked, holding his breath in horror of Winona's answer.

"If I loved him and if he loved Jesus. Jesus says that we should love our enemies." she replied.

One Loon rushed from the *tipi* as if he were choking for air. Almost forgotten were the good memories of the hunt and almost lost were his good thoughts of the coming spring. His heart, he discovered, was sliced in half. One part of it woke up in the morning expecting the day to be happy and exciting. The other part expected the day to be sad or vexing. That part of his heart groaned at the thought of meeting Dr. Williamson or his sister, called Aunt Jane, and telling them once again that he would not come to their school in the mission lodge. All the families of the returned hunters were being visited and asked to come to the school and to the meetings on the holy day.

Even his uncle-father betrayed him and suggested that he go to the mission school. One Loon's mouth was silent, but his eyes spoke a stubborn *no* and an angry *why*.

"It is a great thing Joseph Renville helped the three missionaries—Thomas Williamson, Stephen Riggs, and Gideon Pond— to do. It is an honor to the Dakotas to have their language on the talking leaves. Does a Dakota not do honor to his language by learning to read and to write it? Indeed, my son, it would be wise for us to learn to read and to write the white man's language."

Now the *why* in One Loon's eyes was even angrier!

"Not all white men are praying men like Dr. Williamson," answered Red Beaver. "Not all white men are true-hearted. Many of them speak with forked tongues and tell us lies. Dakota men should be able to read what the white men write on papers and ask us to put our mark to. Ten years ago the Mdewakantonwan chiefs went to Washington and put their marks on paper. Not one of them was able to read what was written on that paper!"

What Red Beaver said was true, of course, but some truths are unwanted and are more vexing than mosquitoes and deer flies. This time One Loon shooed away the vexing truth by asking to go along with Uncida and She Gathers Huckleberries to the sugar camp.

"You are a bit too old to drive away rabbits and chipmunks from the sweet sap," said Red Beaver, a twinkle in his eyes.

"I go as a protector," said One Loon. "I will guard the sugar camp from the Ojibways."

When One Loon and the sugar makers returned to Kaposia nothing more was said about school. The ears of Uncida and One Loon heard nothing but praise for the parfleches stuffed with dark maple and ash sugar and white box elder sugar that Hapanna stored behind the beds. The annoying subject of school did not buzz like a deerfly around his ears again until the Chokecherry Moon. And then school and the beautiful white schoolteacher from the East were the buzzing talk both in Kaposia and the growing village across the Mississippi that was now called St. Paul. Soon every red man and white man up and down the Mississippi and the Minnesota knew that Missionary Williamson had written a letter asking for a female teacher for the children of the new settlers in St. Paul, and a female teacher had come in the person of Miss Harriet Bishop.

One Loon and the whole village watched the new teacher helped ashore by the captain and greeted by the missionaries.

"What laughing thing does the captain say to the white lady?" One Loon asked John Williamson, who had raced to the landing with him.

"He said 'Don't let the Indians scalp you,'" said John, looking uncomfortable.

"That is no laughing thing!" said One Loon curtly.

Nor did One Loon find it a laughing thing that the talk-talk-talk about school and the importance of learning to read and to write was stronger now than ever. Soft-spoken Red Beaver's words clapped his ears like a drum. "For the good of our people you should go to *both* schools. Learn to read and write the Dakota language in the mission school. Learn to read and write the English language in the St. Paul school."

78

For the good of our people I shall seek a vision, One Loon thought to himself. Aloud he said, "For the good of my people I shall seek the true purpose for my life."

"My brother, you can find the true purpose for your life in the Sacred Book," said Winona.

"Tell someone we know," said One Loon to Red Beaver, "that Strong Heart's son is a Dakota, and the true purpose for a Dakota is not in any white man's book!"

12

Great Mystery, Is That All?

But it was Red Beaver who made One Loon's quest for a vision possible. Winona, Hapanna, and even Uncida were not at all cooperative. Winona called it a heathen practice that would send him to the Bad Place.

"Ask someone to tell me where this Bad Place is," said One Loon to Uncida in Winona's presence.

Not bothering to speak through a go-between, Winona pointed downward and said, "My brother, the Bad Place is down there."

"Ask someone to show me the path to the Bad Place!" jeered One Loon. But he was so angry at Winona that he asked John Williamson, who he was beginning to feel could be a brother-friend if he were only a Dakota, what the Sacred Book said about dreams and visions. John asked his Aunt Jane and reported back to One Loon.

Armed with his information One Loon raced to Winona, threw ancient Dakota custom to the winds, looked at her with wide open eyes, and spoke directly to her. "My sister, John Williamson's Aunt Jane says a boy named Joseph had youth visions. She says the white man's great God sent a vision to a Holy Man named John—a great vision that was written down in the white man's Sacred Book. Tell me, my sister, did Joseph and John go to the Bad Place?"

Hapanna's worries were much like Winona's. "My son," she

said, "since you do not walk the Jesus road you might meet bad spirits on your vision quest. They might get you in their power."

Uncida refused to listen to the speculative talk of Winona and Hapanna. Dakota who walked the Good Red Road did not, would not, could not fall into the power of bad spirits! Uncida had her *own* grandmother-worries about One Loon seeking a youth vision. If he went north to find a high place to seek the highest vision, he might fall into the hands of an Ojibway war party. If south, a Sac or Fox war party might surprise him. Uncida wanted him close by and safe.

"My grandson, go to the hill above M'dote," she urged.

"There, my grandmother, I will look across to the white men's fort and the white men's trading posts and the white men's mission lodge. If I look to the east I will see the white men's whiskey town. I must find a high place where I do not look down on white men. The true purpose for my life will have nothing to do with white men," said One Loon firmly.

Red Beaver not only knew such a place but offered to guide One Loon to it, leave him alone there, and come back for him after three sleeps.

"There is a high place on the Standing Rock River near the spot where She Gathers Huckleberries' son and I shot a deer on the winter hunt. It is off the trail to the Wahpekute village near Alexander Faribault's fur-trading post. I shall take you there and go on to visit my brother-friend, War Eagle That May Be Seen."

Red Beaver's words brought gladness to One Loon's heart. He leaped to his feet to run and find his friends, not to tell them that he was going on a vision quest but to tell them he was going on a hunting journey with his uncle-father. It would not be a lie; after all, he would be hunting something.

"Go, my son," said Red Beaver quietly, "but remember that tomorrow you go on a sacred mission. The time for talking much is over. The time to invite the spirit-vision is now."

When One Loon had gone, Red Beaver looked at the ground and said to whatever ears would hear, "When Dakota youth

81

cease to wonder and dream and search, the Dakota nation is dead."

Two sleeps and two days of easy loping on the worn Indian trail brought them to the tall shaft of limestone that gave the river its Dakota name that meant Standing Rock River. Here Red Beaver shot a partridge and roasted it. While they sat and ate, One Loon spoke a thought that had teased his mind ever since they had left Kaposia behind. "My father, we run and do not ride."

"My son, a Dakota changes when he gets on a horse."

"My father, my ears are eager to hear of this change."

"My son, we will talk of that another time. You do not want thoughts chattering like blackbirds in your heart. Visions come most willingly to hearts that are emptied of chattering thoughts."

The sun was well past the middle of the sky when they reached the bluff an arrow's flight from the Indian trail. It was indeed a high place and looked steeply down at the river. Deer droppings hinted that the white-tails used it as a lookout, but there were no signs of human presence. In every way it promised to be a hill of vision.

Before Red Beaver left One Loon to be alone, the sun had nearly reached the edge of the earth. The sweat bath took the in-between time. On the river bottom Red Beaver silently and swiftly built a willow frame and covered it with their two blankets, leaving the opening to the east, the source of light. While One Loon laid a fire, crossing and crisscrossing the sticks at right angles, Red Beaver gathered fist-sized stones from the hillside. These he arranged at the top of the last layer of wood. He lit the fire on the east side, the source of light. In an hour the fire had burned down and the stones were hot. While they sat waiting, Red Beaver saw the why question in One Loon's eyes. "My father, why do we take a sweat bath before seeking a vision?"

"A sweat bath makes brave, my son. A sweat bath removes bad odors and invites the spirits. A sweat bath brings newness."

With two strong forked green saplings, Red Beaver moved the hot stones into the sweat lodge. It was scarcely big enough for the two of them and the pile of hot stones, and when the water hissed on the rocks and the sweat stung his eyes One Loon violently wished to escape. But he did not move until Red Beaver had raised the blanket four times and they went to bathe their copper red bodies in the river. When he rose from the water and climbed to the shore, One Loon felt he could fly if he merely spread his arms.

Before Red Beaver left One Loon to be alone, he took something from his medicine pouch. One Loon recognized it at once as his father's pipe. From the stem hung the long wing feather of an eagle and four strips of skin painted blue, white, red, and yellow for the four directions of the earth. After holding the pipe first to the east, then to the south, then to the north, and then to the west, Red Beaver lifted it to the heavens, then stopped and held it to Mother Earth. As he did so, he prayed a prayer in a low monotone.

> *Hee—ay—hay—ee—ee!*
> *Hee—ay—hay—ee—ee!*
> *Hee—ay—hay—ee—ee!*
> *Hee—ay—hay—ee—ee!*
> Wakantanka, Great Spirit, Grandfather!
> You are first and always have been.
> Everything belongs to you.
> You are one and alone,
> and to you we are sending our voice.
> Be merciful to this, my son.
> Give him a vision to share with our nation.
> Give him a vision true.
> Give him the power to walk in a sacred manner.
> Give him the strength to walk the hard road ahead.

Before Red Beaver left One Loon to be alone, he gave him the pipe. "Your father gave this to me to give to you at this time. When you pray, present it to the four directions of the earth, to the Great Mystery Above, to our Mother the Earth."

When Red Beaver had disappeared, One Loon suddenly felt like a small boy inside his tall, strong, almost-man body, and the

83

small boy wanted to call to his uncle-father, to call him back. But he did not. After the sweat bath, he had felt as if he were afloat in mystery and on the way to a great and telling vision. Now he felt only loneliness and emptiness.

"Wakantanka, Great Mystery, Grandfather!" his heart cried. "Where are you? Up in the sky? Down below? In the clouds? In the storms? Hear me! Pity me! See how pitiful I am!"

What if nothing happened? What if no vision came, no message, no new power? Of one thing he was sure. If nothing happened, if no vision came, he would not lie about it. He would never do as his friend Scabby Wolf at Lac qui Parle had done. When nothing happened on his vision quest, Scabby Wolf had returned and told the Holy Man that he had seen a wolf, a blue wolf—no, a red wolf, a big, red wolf—and the wolf was picked up in a whirlwind and carried away, far away, far far away. When he told the Holy Man his lie-vision, the Holy Man had looked at him for a long time and said, "Scabby Wolf!" From that time on everyone called him Scabby Wolf.

A bitten moon well up in the prairie of the sky shone down on the river and turned it into a bright ribbon. One Loon's eyes followed the ribbon as far as they could see. What kind of a vision would he be granted? A hero vision? A mighty deed vision? The vision of a wolf-spirit or bear-spirit to be his protector? A vision of a mighty stag with antlers like the branches of a great oak? An antelope whose hoofs made the earth tremble? Or a great golden eagle with wings as wide as the Lac qui Parle? The vision of a blue horse with lightning darting from its eyes and from its nostrils?

Yiya! Hiya! No, no! No thunder being vision! No flashing lightning, no rumbling thunder mixed up in his dream vision, for then he would have to become a *heyoka,* a village clown, someone who is never taken seriously, someone the lowliest in the village could tease and torment. Forevermore he would have to do everything backward: wear moccasins on his hands and walk on his hands, ride his horse facing the tail, wear his clothes backward, wear his heaviest blanket in summer and go almost naked in winter, talk backward, say that boiling water is freez-

84

ing, say that rising steam is a cold north wind, weep when everyone laughs, laugh when everyone weeps, walk through a puddle of water and act as if he were drowning. . . .

If he dreamed of thunder and lightning in his youth vision, he would have to become the *heyoka* who protected the band from the perils of lightning with his crazy antics. Perhaps if the *heyoka* at Lac qui Parle had been along with his father and the other leaders on that journey to the sacred pipestone quarry, perhaps the lightning would not have struck them! But who wanted to be a *heyoka* the rest of his life! Who wanted to be a contrary!

But he must stop thinking of lightning and thunder. Perhaps that was what his uncle-father had feared for him when he told him to empty his heart of chattering thoughts!

One Loon held on to the sacred pipe and forced himself to stay awake, but shortly after the noon of night he lay down and fell asleep. To eat and to drink were forbidden on the vision quest, but not sleeping. But he was up and standing erect when the morning star came up. He stood waiting for the sun, holding his father's sacred pipe up to it. "Grandfather Sun, I will not drop my arms until my vision comes!"

When the sun rode high and hot and he could not hold his arms up any longer, he stretched them out to the other directions of the earth. Again and again throughout that long hot day he presented his pipe to the four winds of the earth, to the Mystery Above, to his Mother the Earth. Again and again he prayed, "Wakantanka, have mercy on me! Grant me a vision for the good of my people!"

In late afternoon, his naked body burning with the heat, he fell upon the coolness of the grass and lay outstretched. "Wakantanka, have pity on me! See how pitiful I am!"

Rising to his feet, One Loon once more stretched his pipe to the sun, sliding toward the west. Ah, if only it would travel faster! The moon was already in the sky waiting for night, but it could not be waiting as fiercely as he waited for the coolness of the evening, or more fiercely than he waited for his vision. When his vision had not come by the time the sun rolled off the

85

earth and the white fire bugs were flitting around him, he dropped again to the ground. "*Ina Maka! Ina Maka!* Mother Earth, hear me!"

When Mother Earth did not seem to listen, he cried into the darkness, the loneliness, the emptiness, "*Ate! Ate!* Father! Father!" And he fell asleep.

When One Loon awoke on the second full day of his vision quest, his instant shame at having fallen asleep was quickly driven away by the beautiful sunrise. Where the sky rubbed against the earth the fleecy fair-weather clouds were tinted like a wild rose. One Loon suddenly remembered what Uncida had told him, that every dawn was a holy event and an answer to prayer. "Thank you! Thank you for coming again!" he cried to the sun.

The teeth in his stomach were biting at the emptiness there, but his heart no longer fretted at its hunger for a vision. In fact, all that long day he did not watch for something in the sky and did not once pray, "Come, O come! Come, Holy Vision, come!" All that day he held on to the pipe and watched and listened to his small relatives—ants, grasshoppers, butterflies, the whirr of a rising partridge, the gleam of a crow's wing. "*Mitakuya Owasin!* I am a relative to all!" his heart sang. When a bank swallow swooped past him and dropped a brown feather on his foot, he laughed aloud and winged a thank you to his small relative in its tunnel in the river bank. That night he did not fall asleep but watched the night sky. *The Road of Spirits—the great milky road across the night sky—was his father's spirit in that great crowd? Was his father's spirit watching him this night?*

When that night, his third night alone, was quite old but not quite gone, One Loon's vision came. It came so quickly and was so different from what he had expected that he was not sure of what it actually said until many years later when it finally was fulfilled. Holding his sacred pipe, he had just completed his solemn circle of prayer when he saw it happen as in a dream. Suddenly the space that fell from the cliff to the river burst into a huge fire, the kind of fire white men make. Suddenly the huge leaping fire in his vision died down to a bed of cold, dead ashes.

86

Two shadow-figures knelt on opposite sides of the ugly bed of ashes. Gradually the two shadowy forms became clear and he saw that they were a Dakota youth and a white youth. They were he himself—and John Williamson! With deliberately slow and exaggerated motions, John Williamson stood on his hands, hands that were shod with white men's clumsy shoes, and walked slowly around the dead ash heap, waving his feet in the air. John Williamson was performing the *heyoka* ceremony! John Williamson was a *heyoka!* He circled the ugly ash heap and drew near to the other shadow-figure, the Dakota boy, One Loon himself! To One Loon's horror, he saw his own shadow-figure rise up on moccasinned hands and follow John around the ash heap, waving his feet in the air. He, too, was performing the *heyoka* ceremony! As they danced, there grew from the center of the ash heap a slender cottonwood. The two *heyoka* figures righted themselves and suddenly changed to naked Sun Dancers attached by rawhide thongs to the Holy Tree and to the skewers under the skin of their breasts. With faces lifted to the sun and bodies leaning away from the Sun Dance pole, they danced around the Holy Tree. The Dakota youth—One Loon himself— and the white youth—John Williamson—were dancing the sacred Sun Dance!

The vision faded and vanished, but One Loon was still there, as real as the pebble on the ground that was grating his knee. *Was this his youth vision, then?* Something told him that it was indeed. But if it really was his youth vision, then why was he not trembling? Why was his heart not pounding? Why was his blood not racing through his body? Why did he not feel like singing a song of greatness? Why did he not feel like doing great deeds, giving away great gifts to the poor and the old?

One Loon stretched his arms to the fading stars. "Wakantanka, Great Mystery, Grandfather, *is that all?"*

13

How Does One Become a Warrior Without a War?

"My father, that was all it was. There was no more!" mourned One Loon that evening when he and Red Beaver camped again where the rock stands up and he had told him his vision. "It is nothing to tell the Holy Man. It is nothing to paint on a flag of fawn skin. It is nothing to give a feast for."

"We did not speak of your vision quest to the Holy Man," said Red Beaver. To be honest, Red Beaver did not respect the Holy Man at Kaposia, having sometimes seen him drunk—not with spirit but with the white man's spirit water. "We do not need to tell him your vision. But do not think it is not a good vision, my son! My heart tells me that it foretells something true. Whether good or bad, I do not know."

Nevertheless, One Loon continued to be disappointed in his vision, for he had expected it to give him strength, power, and purpose for becoming a warrior. The time for him to become a warrior was *now*. Right now! Until he had done a manly deed he could not be a man, get a man-name, smoke the sacred pipe with the men, wear eagle feathers like a man. And manly deeds were done in battle!

After his return from his vision quest, One Loon watched his vision-brother, John Williamson, with the eyes of an eagle. He certainly did not see in John a doer of manly deeds, a growing warrior. Taking his sister Nancy Jane and Snana, the Dakota girl who lived with the Williamsons, on canoe rides! According to Winona, John was learning from his mother how to cook and to bake! Carrying water from the river for the women! Milking the mission cows and shoveling manure! Carrying wood! Making fires! Walking through the village with his father and his Aunt Jane and singing to the old ones, the sick ones—although One Loon had to admit that they were strangely beautiful songs, these praise songs to the white men's great god that the missionaries had put into the Dakota language.

Yet One Loon's vision brother was no woman-man in the games they played. Because he was a white boy, the Dakota boys were constantly testing his mettle. They wrestled more roughly with him, tumbled him more savagely in their games. They had to admit grudgingly, however, that he had the strength and staying power of a good Dakota youth.

One Loon's keeping watch on his vision-brother ended with the end of the warm and hazy second summer when the gopher takes a long last look back. Dr. Williamson and his family took the last steamer down the Mississippi that year and went back to Ohio for the winter, leaving the mission work in the hands of other missionaries who had come to help.

"My sister-friend, why does Dr. Williamson go away?" One Loon asked Snana after the steamer had disappeared and the waving and wailing of the Christian Dakota women had stopped.

"He goes to find a home and school for John and Andrew," sniffed Snana. "Aunt Jane has taught them all she knows. John and Andrew will not be coming back with Dr. Williamson when the grass greens again!" Snana burst out wailing all over again.

So now he was gone, his vision-brother who had the strength and staying power of a warrior and the heart of a woman and yet he was not a woman-man. *Hiya!* No, that he was not!

In the hope of being noticed by the warriors in the Kaposia band, One Loon began to hang around the warrior lodge. Here, too, he was disappointed, for the members of the lodge spent much of their time playing cards, gambling, and drinking. In his disappointment he sought out the old men. Week after week that winter he listened wide-eyed to their stories of Dakota deaths avenged, of prisoners taken, of prisoners tortured and even skinned alive.

"Skinned alive?" asked One Loon, his skin prickling.

"Our chief had it done to teach us young braves three lessons," said Broken Hand, an old warrior with white hair. "First, that it could happen to us if we were taken prisoner. Second, that a Dakota warrior is brave but not foolish. He seeks to kill or capture the enemy but he does not seek to be killed or captured by the enemy. Third . . ."

Broken Hand fell silent. One Loon waited, knowing that a Dakota youth does not interrupt or prod an old one in his speaking.

"Third, to set an example to us young warriors. The prisoner that was skinned alive did not make one cry of pain. To his last breath he threw words of scorn at us."

Because Uncida and She Gathers Huckleberries had lived 60 winters they had many brave-heart and glory-in-battle stories to tell on the long winter nights in the *tipi*.

"You should not tell my son such stories," whispered Hapanna, bending low over the moccasin she was making for One Loon.

"My daughter, you are losing the trails of your people!" said Uncida sternly. "My grandson is growing a warrior heart. My grandson will avenge the killing of his grandfather."

"My *hunka*-daughter," said She Gathers Huckleberries, "if your son does not count coup, the men of the warrior lodge will never ask him to join them and the women will whisper about him."

The words of She Gathers Huckleberries struck a chill in One Loon's heart. In his secret thoughts that winter he made up songs and sang them to himself.

> I, too, will do great deeds
> when my time has come,
> when my time has come.
> I, too, will be praised
> when my time has come,
> when my time has come.

Sensing that One Loon's blood was boiling for some desperate and violent deed, Red Beaver one day told him what dark suffering had come upon the Wahpekute band at Alexander Faribault's fur-trading post on the Standing Rock River. It all came because a subchief had been *too* warlike. When the chief, The Cane, reproved Black Eagle for keeping the little band perpetually in conflict with the Ojibways, the Sacs, and the Fox by his vicious activities on the warpath, Black Eagle flew into a rage and killed The Cane, the chief of the Wahpekute band! Banished from the band, Black Eagle took his relatives and fled. Dakotas banished from other bands, banished by their own relatives, joined his band. When Black Eagle died, his son Inkpaduta became the chief of the band of banished Dakota. War Eagle That May Be Seen was made the new chief of the Wahpekute band on the Standing Rock River.

"Open your ears, my son, and hear what happened to War Eagle, my brother-friend. On a hunting party on the Blue Earth River, War Eagle and his men, 17 in number, were stabbed to death in their sleep by Inkpaduta and his band of. . . . Of what, my son? Shall we call them Dakota warriors or Dakota murderers?"

In the Grass-Greening Moon 34 warriors from the village where the Standing Rock River flowed into the Mississippi came up the Mississippi on a war party and were joined by 16 Kaposian warriors. One Loon had fiercely hoped to be invited along as a moccasin boy. When the war party returned, they had 14 Ojibway scalps and one prisoner. The village of Kaposia went wild with joy and danced the scalp dance for many nights. The women danced, too, tonguing the tremolo in a high voice. One Loon painted his body with his own designs, for he was as yet unproven, hung rattles made of the dewclaws of deer on his ankles, and danced to the beating drums. But only the first night. When he discovered that Red Beaver stayed away from the scalp dance he could not keep from asking why, even though he knew prying questions were not courteous.

"My son asks me why I do not dance a victory dance for the 14 Ojibway scalps. My son, they are the scalps of 14 old men, women, and children surprised in a sugar camp. The great Dakota victory was killing a band of helpless Ojibways made more helpless by the white man's whiskey. They were drunk, my son. My son's father does not dance to such a victory!"

But a month later even Red Beaver's heart flamed with revenge. Accompanied by two or three of his warriors, Hole-in-the-Day, the young chief of the Ojibway tribe, came down the Mississippi River, hid his canoe in the gorge leading to the cave, and stealthily scouted for unsuspecting Dakotas. They surprised and attacked a small party of them and vanished upriver as quickly as they had come. Behind them they left one dead scalped Dakota. It was the son of She Gathers Huckleberries. It was not Taopi, who had already been wounded in a previous battle with the Ojibway. It was the one with whom Red Beaver had hunted on the Standing Rock River.

That night every able-bodied man and youth in Kaposia painted for war, danced to the drum, and shouted war cries. That night Red Beaver and One Loon danced and shouted:

Hi! Hi! Hi! Hi—ah—ee—ah!
Go we now! Go we now!
Go in anger! Go in anger!
Scalps to get! Scalps to get!

In the morning a long line of 50 or more Dakota warriors, painted and stripped for battle, ran through the streets of St. Paul on their way to Ojibway territory, crying, *"Hu—ka—he! Hu—ka—he!"* Miss Harriet Bishop's schoolchildren shrieked in terror and clung to their teacher's skirts. In the dark of the night a long line of Dakota warriors straggled back through the streets of St. Paul, shooting their guns in the air to vent their anger and frustration at finding no Ojibways to scalp. It was One Loon's first going on the warpath. Not one bullet or arrow whizzed by his ears, and he made no glory for himself, but nobody could say that he had been afraid.

Ever since the white people had declared the land east of the Mississippi together with the land acquired from the Dakota on the west bank to be Minnesota Territory and named Alexander

92

Ramsey its governor, the number of white people pouring into that territory had increased alarmingly. But if the surge of whites into St. Paul and elsewhere alarmed the Dakota, their alarm was nothing compared to the alarm of the white people over the renewed bloodshedding between the Dakotas and the Ojibways.

In the Moon When the Strawberries Are Red Governor Ramsey called the two warring tribes to a council meeting outside the gates of Fort Snelling. The governor and many of the leading citizens of St. Paul and the new territory, some of them accompanied by their wives, were present. A troop of fully armed soldiers stood at attention. Other soldiers stood beside the huge mounted gun the Dakota called *woope*. Chief Hole-in-the-Day arrived with two hundred warriors and headmen. All of them waited for the Dakota. The sun was well past the middle before a lone horseman galloped up to announce that the Dakota would not come until the next day.

On the following morning all were assembled before the gates of Fort Snelling again—but still no Dakota! The sun was high in the sky before they saw a long line of horsemen approaching at furious speed. They rode past, wheeled, discharged their guns, and dismounted. Governor Ramsey ordered all guns to be stacked against the walls of the fort. The Dakota were seated, and the council finally began.

But after the pipe had been passed and smoked, Little Crow arose to protest the presence of the white women. "The Dakota have come to meet in council with the Ojibway—not with women!"

"The Dakota did not object to the presence of women, even children, in the massacre of the Ojibways in April!" answered Governor Ramsey acidly. Then Chief Hole-in-the-Day declared himself happy to see so many sweet women there and shook hands with Mrs. Ramsey and the other white women present.

That evening Red Beaver laughingly reported all this to his family. "It is easy to see who lost *that* battle—Chief Little Crow, whose greatest ambition is to be popular!"

After three days of meeting, the two tribes made peace and

were told by Governor Ramsey that in the future breakers of the peace would be tried and punished by the laws of the Territory. Red Beaver, somewhat more soberly, reported that, too, at home. One Loon was dismayed.

"My father, if that is so, how can we avenge the son of She Gathers Huckleberries? Will his spirit forever wander unavenged?"

And how can I ever walk in my father's moccasins and become a warrior? he thought to himself. *How can I ever do a manly deed? What do warriors do when there is no war?* he thought—and for a moment felt like testing his bravery by standing in the coals of a dying cooking fire.

Even with the tension, excitement, and challenge of the ancient enmity between the Dakota and Ojibway dampened temporarily, the rest of the summer proved eventful. Dr. Williamson and his family—minus John and Andrew, as Snana had predicted—had returned in the Planting Moon. In midsummer all the brother-and-sister missionaries gathered at Little Crow's village for a great council meeting. From far away Lac qui Parle and Traverse des Sioux they came across the prairie in canvas-covered ox carts laden with wives, children, cooking pots, food, and beds. Hapanna and Winona rose before dawn to do their own daily tasks at home and spent the rest of the day helping the white missionary wives with the children and the feeding of the great gathering. One Loon and Uncida had never seen Winona so happy.

"My granddaughter, you act as if they are all blood relatives!" grumbled Uncida.

"My grandmother, they are more than that! They are my Jesus-relatives!"

Later that summer Uncida and One Loon saw Winona even happier. She had finally found her true love, a true love who had had the saving waters poured on his head, received the name of Moses, and worshiped the white man's great god and son-of-god. Gray Whirlwind was his Dakota name, and a fit one it was, for his courtship of Winona was a whirlwind courtship. He was a Wahpetonwan from Lac qui Parle and had come

94

along with the missionary Huggins' family to help them on the journey. Hapanna remembered how Strong Heart had also come from the Wahpetonwan village on the Lac qui Parle and wooed and won her here in Little Crow's village.

Red Beaver and One Loon went hunting for meat for the wedding feast. It was One Loon who first saw the antelope, and it was One Loon who shot him, but it was Red Beaver who showed him how to crawl through the grass, circle the antelope until the sun was at their backs and blinded the animal's vision.

"Antelope," he whispered, "are the wariest of animals. See how one of them always has its head in the air watching for danger."

Of course the Jesus-relatives as well as the blood-relatives and the *hunka*-relatives were invited to the feast after the wedding ceremony at the mission lodge. One Loon could not help noticing that most of the Dakota Jesus-relatives were women. There were very few Dakota men with cut hair and wearing white men's clothes. The next time he was alone with Red Beaver he asked him why Dakota women said yes to the white men's religion and the Dakota men said no.

Red Beaver answered so swiftly that One Loon knew he must have thought this matter out in his heart many times. "It is because the Dakota man has to give up everything that makes him a Dakota man, my son! He gives up fighting. He gives up smoking the sacred pipe. He gives up his nakedness, for the missionaries think it shameful. He gives up the blanket, for he has to work with his hands. He gives up his long hair. He gives up feasts. He gives up the drums and the dancing. If he has more than one wife, he gives them up. He gives up his freedom to do as he pleases on the holy day. To ask a Dakota man to walk the Jesus road is like asking the buffalo to live as a beaver.

"Yet," he added after a silence, "the few Dakota men who have chosen to walk on the Jesus road are not nor ever were women-men. They have been some of the bravest Dakota warriors. But even the brave ones stumble and fall. Do you remember Aniwegamani?"

"Simon Cut Hair?" asked One Loon.

"My ears have heard that he has been put out of the mission

95

church for drunkenness. The white man's whiskey has made a fool of him."

"The white man's religion made a fool of him *first*," said One Loon curtly.

There was another event that summer. How eventful it was no one realized at the time. The Kaposians were becoming quite accustomed to steamboats loaded with curious white people from the East coming up the river to see the Falling Waters of the Mississippi. More and more of them tramped through Little Crow's village. Some of them asked prying questions through interpreters and wrote things on talking leaves. Uncida stubbornly refused to give them her memories.

She Gathers Huckleberries cheerfully gave them *her* memories —and just as cheerfully asked for money. "Sometimes," she confided to Uncida, "I make them up. I told the last white man that two braves fought each other and died for me when I was a maiden."

The event that summer that was so portentful to the Dakota people was the chartering of the temperance and sabbath-keeping steamer *Nominee* by a large group of summer tourists and prominent citizens of St. Paul, Fort Snelling, and Mendota for an excursion up the Minnesota River to the farthest point yet reached by steamer. It was a noisy and colorful crowd that boarded the *Nominee* at St. Paul. One Loon and his friends watched the boarding and followed the steamer on shore to Mendota, where another crowd got on. The Fort Snelling band marched on board playing lively music. For almost everyone on board this was the first view of the great beautiful valley of the Minnesota. But not all the passengers had eyes just for the beauty. In the time allotted on shore, the men fingered the soil and pronounced it the richest they had ever seen.

When the steamer turned around at about the hundred-mile point, a spontaneous "convention" was called, to which the ladies were invited. Speeches were made and a resolution enthusiastically and unanimously adopted recommending that a treaty for the Minnesota Valley be quickly made with the eastern bands of the Dakota. "These lands ought and must be ours!"

96

14

Fuel for the Conflagration

The white people lost no time in gaining possession of the lands—the immense and immensely fertile valley of the Minnesota River. They acquired it by means of two treaties in the summer of 1851. The first was made at Traverse des Sioux between the U. S. government and the Sisseton and Wahpetonwan bands of the Dakota nation. The second was made at Mendota between the U. S. government and the Mdewakontanwan and Wahpekute bands of the Dakota nation.

Because Red Beaver was a Wahpetonwan Dakota and because Hapanna and Uncida had lived so long at the Wahpetonwan village on the Lac qui Parle and had so many Wahpetonwan friends, they packed their *tipi* and kettle and few belongings on a pony drag and went to the great gathering of the Sissetons and Wahpetonwans at Traverse des Sioux. Winona and her Wahpetonwan Christian husband Moses Gray Whirlwind and the baby girl they now had also accompanied the little band of travelers. Most of them, One Loon observed, were Christian Dakota who had moved to Kaposia when Dr. Williamson had come there five winters ago. It was not hard to tell the Christian Dakota men, for only they would help put up *tipis* and make fires and carry water. One Loon soon learned that Winona's baby was not the only woman-child named after Aunt Jane, the Red Song Woman. There were at least three little Dakota Janes in the group that camped together on the journey.

"But what is her Dakota name?" Uncida had asked Winona after the Naming Feast that Winona called baptism.

"My grandmother, she is a child of Jesus and needs but one name," answered Winona.

"*Hou—u—un!*" murmured Uncida in regret.

The steamer *Excelsior* carried the white men up the river to the meeting. Governor Ramsey and Luke Lea, commissioner of Indian affairs, came as the officials appointed by the U.S. government to purchase the land. Long Trader Sibley from Mendota and Henry Rice from St. Paul were along, as well as James Madison Goodhue from the St. Paul newspaper and reporters from other newspapers all over the United States. Dr. Thomas Williamson, carrying enough medicines to set up a small apothecary shop, was along as physician for the huge encampment. The Minnesota River was high, but the boat rode low with its load of people, food for the whole assemblage, and the bawling herd of cattle in the hold.

Couriers had been sent to all the Wahpetonwan and Sisseton bands. For two weeks the bands dribbled in day after day, band by band, with carts and pony drags. A band of Sissetons from above the Lac qui Parle presented themselves to the commissioners with a flare and a flourish, singing war songs and beating drums. When the Lac qui Parle band came and set up their *tipis*, the Kaposian-Wahpetonwans moved their *tipis* into their circle and set up camp with them. Every morning each band sent a delegation to the commissioners' camp to get beef, rice, and flour for the day's cooking and tobacco for the day's smoking.

One Loon came along with his family for one reason and one high hope only—to see his *koda*-friend Jean Baptiste Renville once again. When he could not find him in the noise and confusion of the arrival of the Lac qui Parle band, when the others were finding blood-and-*hunka*-relatives on every side, One Loon, his heart on the ground, wandered to the river. And there he was —Jean Baptiste, as tall and straight and slim as himself. He was watering his horse and rubbing it down. One Loon moved like a shadow to the other side of the horse and began rubbing it

98

down as well. The two pair of eyes met over the horse's back, slid shyly away, and then met again in unconcealed joy. From that moment until the breaking of camp they were together from the time morning stood up until the night was old and they went to sleep. But even in sleep they were as close as brother-friends could be, for they quickly made their own shelter of poles and brush and spread their blankets inside. By the time the council meeting was over, the aspen leaves of their shelter had turned brown and rustled in the wind.

By keeping their ears and eyes open One Loon and Jean Baptiste soon learned that the whites were planning a great feast to honor and celebrate something. Was it to celebrate the birthday of the Grandfather in Washington? Or was it to honor and celebrate the red-white-and-blue piece of cloth that seemed to be as all-meaningful a symbol to them as the pipe was to the Dakotas? They were not sure, but of one thing they were sure: this day in the Chokecherry Moon was a special day for the white people. Robert Hopkins, who was the missionary at Traverse des Sioux and from whose well all the whites drew water for themselves, was to lead all in prayer to the great god. There would be music by the Fort Snelling band. There would be buffalo meat, boiled ham, and beef.

But the day for celebration became a black day of mourning instead. Missionary Hopkins went out early to bathe in the river and never returned. His clothes were found on the bank, but his body was not found for two days.

One Loon and Jean Baptiste joined the searchers for the body —the stunned and grief-silent missionaries, the grim-faced white officials and soldiers, the Christian Indians trying to hobble their grief, the other Indians crying theirs out loudly as do most of Wakantanka's creatures in the first anguish of loss.

Because One Loon and Jean Baptiste could swim like pike, they dove into the river and swam under water, searching out the deep dark places where a limp and lifeless body could hide. After hours of fruitless searching near the place where it was thought Robert Hopkins had drowned, they walked downstream and scanned the water and shoreline with the eyes of hawks.

99

Black gnats and mosquitoes rose in clouds around their heads. The high water lapped at the tree roots, and the gurgling and chuckling sounded ominously to One Loon's ears as if the waters of the river were jeering at them.

"My brother, something tells me that Unkte'h, the god of the waters, is angry with the missionaries. He has now taken two of them here at Traverse des Sioux. First the brother of Missionary Rigg's wife. Now this missionary. Unkte'h must be trying to tell the missionaries to go away and leave his Dakota children alone."

"Superstition!" snorted Jean Baptiste.

"My brother uses a word my ears do not know," said One Loon.

"There are no other gods but the one true and great god. To believe anything else is superstition."

"My brother has gone too long to the mission school," said One Loon, but he said it with a smile, for he did not want anything to cloud the sky of this friendship. Since Jean Baptiste felt the same way, neither of them spoke again of gods and spirits in that time together.

To be honest, it must be said that after the missionary's body floated to the surface and was buried under the ground, most of the whites and the Dakota seemed to forget that anything sad had happened. While the commissioners waited for all the Wahpetonwans and Sissetons to arrive, the Dakota bands that were already there entertained themselves and their white hosts by riding around on horses and shooting blank cartridges by day and with war dances at night. There also was a wedding to which everyone was invited. Nancy McClure, a shy, 14-year-old half-breed girl One Loon remembered from Lac qui Parle, was married to young David Faribault, son of Jean Baptiste Faribault, the fur trader at Mendota. The bride trembled all through the ceremony and did not even lift her eyes when the commissioners loudly toasted her with lemonade.

"The young husband is not much older than we are," chuckled Jean Baptiste. "Do you ever think of taking a wife, my brother?"

In a voice so low that Jean Baptiste could scarcely hear it,

100

One Loon answered, "Not a drop of my blood shall ever flow in any child-woman or child-man!"

"My brother!" exclaimed Jean Baptiste, "why do you say such a strange thing? Is your heart on the ground? Have you played the flute to someone and she has not come out to you and stood under your blanket with you?"

"My brother!" exclaimed One Loon passionately, pointing to the crowd of thousands of Indians with a sweep of his arm. "They are like ducks dancing with their eyes closed. They are like children laughing and dancing in the village circle while a great grass fire is sweeping across the prairie and is about to burn them all. They marry and shoot their guns off and dance as if what is happening here is not going to affect them for the rest of their lives! They marry and shoot their guns and dance as if they are not about to be pushed down the Road of Hardship! As for their dancing, my brother," One Loon went on bitterly, "no longer do our people dance in the sacred way. They dance for entertainment, their own and the whites'! They dance to please men they do not see as their worst enemies."

After two weeks of waiting, all the Sisseton and Wahpetonwan bands had arrived and the talking began under the great aspen arbor the Long Knives had built. One Loon and Jean Baptiste watched the white leaders and the Dakota chiefs through the smoke of smudges built to keep away the gnats and mosquitoes, but they of course could not get close enough to hear what was being said. However, the Dakota chiefs came back to their camps at night and talked with their council. Ears listened and tongues talked. Truths, half-truths, and rumors flew from *tipi* to *tipi*, chattering like little birds in the spring. Late at night, stretched out on their blankets in their shelter, One Loon and Jean Baptiste tried to separate the true from the untrue, somewhat as Dakota women shake the chaff out of the wild rice. Sometimes the stars began to fade before they fell asleep.

"Before my father died," said Jean Baptiste one night, "he said that he hoped the white people would be satisfied with the land east of the Father of Waters and would not cross it. But now," he sighed, "now they come and say, 'Move a little farther.

101

Go a little farther! We will make a little island on the prairie for you to live on and you can live there as long as the grass grows and the rivers run.'"

"Hear what Uncida said to us while we ate soup tonight. Uncida said that we cannot give this land to the whites in exchange for money any more than we can give them the air or the lakes or the clouds in exchange for money. Everything belongs to Wakantanka and is shared by all the creatures, the two-leggeds and the four-leggeds. Wakantanka put the Dakota on this place. This is the place where Wakantanka wants the Dakota nation to live."

"Hear what else Uncida said," One Loon went on. "She said that every part of this land is sacred. Every hill, every valley, every stream, every forest, every lake and pond and swamp. The whites plow deep and bring hurt and harm to the breast of our Mother the Earth. They will destroy the sacred kinship the Dakota have with this land. Uncida was so sad that she could not eat the meat and went to her blanket weeping and saying over and over, 'We do not care for another place. This is our home. We want this place and no other!'"

Another long night they talked about where the white people wanted to move the four eastern bands of the Dakota nation.

"My brothers tell me that it will be a narrow strip of prairie on both sides of the Minnesota River beginning at Lac qui Parle and ending before the Big Bend," said Jean Baptiste. "The commissioners call them reservations."

"Do they think that they can compel Dakota people to stay on one small narrow place and not move freely about? They can just as well ask buffalo to stay on their reservations!" said One Loon scornfully. "And what do they expect us to do on their reservations? Sit in *tipis* and talk and smoke and grow big bellies?"

"I think they expect us to become white people. I think they want us to dig the earth and plant corn and grow cattle," said Jean Baptiste.

One Loon sat up so suddenly his head almost went through the low roof of aspen branches over their shelter. "Who are they to ask the Dakotas to change their ways? Do they know more than Wakantanka? Did they make the world? Do they make the grass grow? Wakantanka made them to wear clothes, to plow, to shovel manure, to eat tame cow and tame geese. Wakantanka made the Dakota to go naked, to roam, to hunt, to eat wild geese and buffalo."

"Maybe there is no other way," said Jean Baptiste softly. "Maybe, my brother, maybe the Dakota *have* to change!"

"My brother, do *you* want to walk the same road as the white men?" whispered One Loon.

Jean Baptiste sighed from far below his ribs. "My brother, I do not know! I search the thoughts of my heart and do not know!"

The Dakota chiefs and the commissioners argued and argued. Two chiefs, Red Iron and Sleepy Eye, opposed the treaty and refused to sign. When the food was almost gone and they foresaw the plight of the thousands of Dakota in the encampment, they gave in.

"Whenever we do not agree," they said bitterly, "we get the same answer. 'You will get no more food.'"

The treaty of Traverse des Sioux was signed with the Wahpetonwan and Sisseton Dakota on July 23, 1851.

The treaty with the Mdewakantonwan and the Wahpekute Dakota was signed at Pilot Knob above Mendota on August 7, 1851.

In both cases gifts of colored blankets, beads, ribbons, cloth, and gun powder were given to the Dakota tribes after the signing. Also a first payment of $30,000 in cash. The second week in August the streets of St. Paul were crowded with Dakota men carrying pouches of double-eagles and buying up every wheezing, spavined cart horse to be had—and whiskey by the keg. Many a Kaposian mother gathered her children and fled to the hills.

On June 26, 1852, the U.S. Senate ratified the two treaties, and the bonfires blazed on the bluffs of St. Paul. Little Crow's village soon learned what the bonfires meant—the Great Father in Washington was going to demand that they move.

On Sunday, July 13, 1852, began the great three-day game in which One Loon earned his man-name, Shakopee's band came to Oak Grove to play lacrosse with Good Road's band. Two to three hundred men took part in the game at some time, and over $4000 worth of goods were wagered. On the third day Little Crow's band joined the game, and it was One Loon who caught the ball in the pocket of his long stick and raced past the goal post and won the game for Shakopee's band. From then on One Loon shed his youth name and was called Inyanka Duza Tanka, Swift Runner. Very soon his man-name was shortened to Kaduza.

But even as One Loon streaked past the goal post that day and heard the roar of the crowd, he remembered what he had said just one year before to his *koda*-friend, Jean Baptiste Renville. "They are like ducks dancing with their eyes closed. They are like children laughing and dancing in the village circle while a great grass fire is sweeping across the prairie about to burn them all."

15

On the Reservation

Dr. Thomas Williamson and his son John, recently returned from school in Ohio, were not at Kaposia to witness the great lacrosse game between the Mdewakantonwan bands clustered near the fort. Neither did they witness the bonfires on the bluffs of St. Paul to celebrate the signing of the two treaties. Never doubting that they would be signed, Dr. Williamson loaded his wagon with tools and supplies and took John and a small crew and started west to build his third mission house since his arrival in Dakota country 17 years before. They followed the old route —by boat to Traverse des Sioux, by wagon across the prairie. The place he selected for the new mission was on the reservation reserved for the Wahpetonwan and Sisseton Dakota, with whom Dr. Williamson expressed a preference to work because they had had less contact with white men. It was on high prairie one mile west of the Minnesota River and a few miles above the place where the Yellow Medicine River joins the Minnesota. He gave his new mission the Dakota name for the river—Pejutazi, Yellow Medicine.

The little party arrived at the site early enough to plant a garden. There in the wilderness they cut logs on the river bottomland and hewed them with an axe. They sawed the joists with a whipsaw. At the end of their long days of labor the bone-weary men sat down to a supper of John's gray soggy dumplings, boiled turnips, and catfish and were grateful to Margaret Williamson for teaching her son John some of the rudiments of cooking.

Winona and her husband and the other Christian Dakota at Kaposia promptly decided that when the Great Father in Washington asked them to move they would go and live near Missionary Williamson at Yellow Medicine. In fact, they might not even wait for the Great Father to tell them to move! To Hapanna's joy, Red Beaver, although not a Christian, seemed willing to live somewhere in the neighborhood of the mission. Winona and Hapanna (tactfully, they thought) had Moses Gray Whirlwind ask Kaduza where he planned to live. "With us, we hope! Or at least *near* us!" they said.

In Kaduza's cold answer his family had their first inkling of the hatred of the whites brewing and distilling in his heart.

"My brother-in-law, the whites have taken away the Dakota man's right to choose where he lives. But if it is allowed to choose between living with Moses and Amos and Jacob and Simon and living with Dakota who want nothing to do with Dakota men who have gotten their names from white missionaries, I choose to live on the little prison island reserved for the Mdewakantonwans and the Wahpekutes. And I shall take Uncida with me."

"My son, Uncida is my mother!" cried Hapanna. "She must come with me."

"My mother, ask her yourself!" said Kaduza sternly.

"My relatives," said Uncida cheerfully when asked, "I have already searched my heart on this matter, and I go gladly with my grandson. My grandson needs someone to cook his soup and to mend his moccasins."

"My son," said Red Beaver sadly to Kaduza when they were alone, "Do not let hatred bring ruin to your heart."

"My father," answered Kaduza, "the missionaries tell my mother and sister that a snake stole to the First Mother and lied to her and brought ruin to all men. My mother and sister will soon learn that the white men are the snake that will bring ruin to the Dakota."

"Are you so new to the world that you think evil was just born

106

and the white man is its father?" asked Red Beaver, his voice rising. "Has my son forgotten that the Wahpekute chief Black Eagle killed his own brother chief, The Cane? Has my son forgotten that Inkpaduta, son of Black Eagle, killed War Eagle That May Be Seen and 17 of his brother Wahpekutes? Not all Dakota are good, my son, and not all the white people are bad."

And so they separated. In their eagerness to be near the beloved Williamson family and the new mission, Hapanna and Winona and some of the other Christian Dakota left Kaposia that autumn and pitched their *tipis* in a small Dakota village about three miles from Yellow Medicine. To their surprise they found Eagle Help, the first Dakota to learn to read—and from Missionary-Doctor Williamson!—living there with his nine children. To their joy they discovered that Eagle Help, who had refused to worship in the mission church at Lac qui Parle, had become a Christian and was going to worship at Yellow Medicine on the Holy Day.

Winter began early and was the coldest and hungriest winter the Dakota had ever known. If it had not been for Eagle Help, who shared his corn with them, and for Dr. Williamson, who gave them the young cow he was saving to give milk in the spring, Kaduza's kin would have died that winter. There was no game on the prairie, and the snow lay so deep on the rivers that fishing through the ice was almost impossible.

In early December Dr. Williamson sent two men with three horses and a yoke of oxen to Traverse des Sioux, a hundred miles across the prairie, to fetch supplies. Having purchased the supplies and another team of oxen, the men started back. On December 13 a blizzard howled out of the north and continued until the end of the month. Supplies were abandoned and finally the horses and oxen as well. Three weeks later the men stumbled home to Yellow Medicine with feet and hands so badly frozen that Dr. Williamson had to amputate the toes of one man and treat the men's painfully damaged limbs all winter long. The mission family of ten people lived that winter on two barrels of flour, a barrel and a half of corn meal, and two barrels of potatoes. Nor

107

would they have had that if missionaries Riggs and Huggins had not sent it down from Lac qui Parle in midwinter.

Kaduza packed his little grandmother and her *tipi* on a pony drag and moved along with Little Crow's village to the land reserved for the Mdewakantonwans and the Wahpekutes. Uncida pitched her *tipi* next to She Gathers Huckleberries, and the two of them promptly found a piece of land on which to plant corn and squash. Both of them had deep sorrow-wounds to heal. Uncida missed her kinfolk more than she dared let Kaduza know. She Gathers Huckleberries had lost another member of her family to the Ojibways. That very spring a sister had been mortally wounded in a surprise attack by the Ojibways on the streets of St. Paul. She Gathers Huckleberries herself had paddled her canoe and brought her dying sister back to Kaposia.

Kaduza, too, had a wound—or rather a psychic shock, to heal. His searching spirit, his open and listening spirit, his child-youth spirit, the spirit that Uncida once said had shot between the horns of the new moon on the *wakan* night he was born, seemed to have fled, and an angry spirit had moved into the other spirit's house, a bitter, restless spirit that made him hate not only the whites but also any Dakota who favored adopting white men's costumes and customs, schools and churches, made him even hate for a time his own mother and sister and Red Beaver, too, who was not a destroyer of the old ways but yet was not hostile to the new ways. With a thorn-apple barb in his humor, Kaduza told Uncida that her son-in-law was like a blackbird sitting on a white farmer's rail fence—its head on one side and its tail on the other.

With the other restless and angry young Mdewakantonwans and Wahpekutes Kaduza rode up and down and across their reservation and saw that it was mostly prairie and that there was no game. On foot and moving as silently as shadows, they slipped back into their old hunting grounds in the land that had been sold to the whites. They saw that their old trails had become the white men's roads. Once when they were near the Standing Rock River Kaduza slipped away from his little band of friends and stayed the night on the bluff where he had sought and had his vision. For hours he gazed moodily down at the river and in mind-pictures saw again the space that fell from the cliff to the river burst into a huge fire and burn to dead ash. He saw again the shadow-figure of John Williamson rise on his hands, shod in shoes, and walk around the ash heap. Saw his own shadow-figure rise on moccasinned hands. He saw the sacred Sun Pole rise out of the ashes, saw himself and John Williamson rise upright and become Sun Dancers around the Sacred Tree. Kaduza pondered the meaning until moon-set but came no closer to understanding his vision.

In the morning Kaduza crept stealthily to the fringe of wood along the old trail, now deep with dust and rutted with cart wheels, and watched the wagons and carts go by on their way to and from St. Paul or Hastings and Alexander Faribault's town. Two stage coaches, 14 yoke of oxen, and so many double teams and single buggies passed by that he grew tired of counting and started for the home that was home only because Uncida was there. It was night when he skirted New Ulm. Since he had found no game, he raided a chicken coop and silenced two fat hens by wringing their necks.

Hearing the squawking in his chicken coop, the farmer came out and shot into the darkness. *"Was zum Teufel! Donnerwetter!"*

Kaduza laughed to himself. Later he picked ears of soft corn from another farmer's field.

"My grandson, did you steal this food?" asked Uncida the next day as they feasted on chicken and corn.

"My grandmother, the white men want us to live and think and do as they do. That must mean that they must want us to eat as they do. If they do not provide, we must take."

"Our old blood creeps like the turtle," sighed Uncida to She Gathers Huckleberries later that day. "Theirs leaps like the cougar. It is too bad that these young ones cannot hunt or go on horse raids or go into battle and still their stormy blood. It is too bad that they cannot live the old Dakota way and learn self-control."

"Your grandson who is close to you can still his stormy young blood and learn self-control by following a plow," said She

109

Gathers Huckleberries tartly, surprising Uncida with both her words and the way she spoke her words. "The Father in Washington is giving Dakota men who give up their old ways and become farmers house and fields, a plow, a wagon, and a team of oxen. My son has chosen to join the farmer Dakota. Your grandson can do the same."

"Your son Taopi?" asked Uncida. "And will your son cut his hair and wear pantaloons?"

"If he does not, my son will not receive gifts from the Father in Washington."

Uncida wondered if it was Taopi's hunger or his heart that influenced his decision. When she told Kaduza about the gifts from their great Father in Washington, Kaduza seized a branch from Uncida's woodpile near the *tipi* opening and broke it into many pieces.

"Our Father in Washington!" he exclaimed. "The Dakota have no father in Washington! My father sits at the Campfire of Spirits where they are weeping for their kinfolk here on earth. Whenever it rains, my heart tells me that it is the water of tears they are weeping for us."

"As for the gifts of the Great Father in Washington," he said, violently breaking another branch, "the white men give the Dakota people nothing! White men have the greed disease and do not know how to give. They can only take, take, take."

It was easy for Uncida to see that the most shaming thing Kaduza had to do was to present himself at the agency to receive payment in gold and provisions from the white men. Twice a year he joined thousands of Dakota and waited for the annuity money, waited for his number to be called so that he could step up to the table flanked by Long Knives from the new Fort Ridgely lower down on the Minnesota River and receive whatever the white people chose to give in provisions, receive whatever gold was left over after the traders had checked their books to see if the Dakota with that number owed them money. Like everyone else, Kaduza had to buy from the traders in a new white way called "buying on credit." But neither he nor any other Dakota man knew what was written in those books. All they knew was

110

that very little gold coin was placed into their hands, and they very soon were forced to buy on credit once again.

Since Kaduza's family was registered with Little Crow's band, they, too, had to come to the Lower Agency for their annuity payments. When Kaduza saw his father with cut hair and white men's clothes for the first time, he swiftly closed his face to him and said nothing for hours. Not until evening when they were outside Uncida's *tipi* did he ask him coldly if he felt like a Dakota brave wearing those ugly clothes.

"My son," answered Red Beaver gently, "clothes are only a wrapping. The wrappings have changed, but the Dakota person inside the wrappings has not changed."

Kaduza's next question came from his heart and not his hate. "My father, it seems that you have chosen to walk the white man's road. Have you also chosen to become a Christian?"

Red Beaver was silent for a long time. "My son, my heart has searched to unwrap the truth deep inside our ancient Dakota religion and the truth deep inside the white man's religion. My heart finds the two truths to be like brothers. But the missionaries say that our religion—its unwrapped truth as well as its wrappings—is from a bad spirit. My heart cannot say yes to that."

Red Beaver lapsed into silence. Kaduza's thoughts slowly lapsed into the same silence, and his ears gradually began to hear what the women were chattering about behind them.

"Uncida," his mother was saying, "do you remember Simon Aniwegamani?"

"The one the boys called Simon Cut Hair?"

"Yes, that one. He fell away from the church because he began drinking the whiskey that makes men fools. He has quit drinking whiskey forever. Simon is back in our church at Yellow Medicine. Simon is a Christian again. *All the way!*"

"Do you remember Eagle Help?" chimed in Winona. "He works harder on his farm than any Dakota man has ever worked. He, too, comes to our church at Yellow Medicine and is a Christian. *All the way!*"

Kaduza leaped to his feet.

"*All the way! All the way!* The white men have gotten our

111

country, but they are not satisfied. They want to force their ways and their religion upon us. *All the way!*"

Kaduza pulled his blanket tightly around his shoulders and stalked out into the darkness. That night he slept out on the open prairie.

16

John Has Come!

It was Uncida who gentled Kaduza through the next few years. It was a relief to come home to her after a day with the young Mdewakantonwan and Wahpekute males, who seemed to have caught the white man's disease of talking too much and too loudly.

Big words and small thoughts, groaned Kaduza to himself on his way home one evening—and suddenly realized how much he missed Red Beaver's big thoughts and small soft-spoken words. But then he had Uncida. Now that She Gathers Huckleberries had gone with her son to join the farmer Dakota, Uncida did her daily work in silence. She greeted Kaduza quietly and wrapped a comfortable silence around him while he ate and stretched out on his buffalo robe. Tonight he found her decorating a new pair of moccasins she had made for him, decorating them with porcupine quills dyed in the paint from the red sumac and the blue spiderwort.

"My grandson," she said cheerily, "I have sat so quietly all day that my feet are beginning to wonder what is the matter with me."

"My grandmother," said Kaduza, "tell your feet that there is nothing the matter with you."

"Little Grandmother," he said an hour later as he lay on his bed on the man-side of Uncida's *tipi*, "it is good to come home from the *tipi* of the big world that has everything the matter with it to a little grandmother's *tipi* that has nothing the matter with it."

One day in his restless roaming and observing on the reservation, Kaduza found Snana, the beautiful Dakota girl who had lived with the Williamson family at Kaposia for four years but had been taken back to her village to live as a Dakota again. Married to Good Thunder at the age of 15, she now lived with her husband on the Lower Reservation, where they were building a log house.

Snana proudly showed him her firstborn. "Is she not beautiful?"

"My sister, a beautiful tree bears beautiful fruit," laughed Kaduza, secretly wishing that Snana had not been taken away from Kaposia before he could have played the flute to her. But, no—Snana, too, was a Christian. Her husband, too, she told him proudly—although she need not have told him. Anyone could see it from his cut hair and white men's clothing.

After the summer when Uncida's tiny field of corn shriveled and died and there was no corn to be bought and no game to be found, Kaduza brought Uncida to her daughter's log lodge near Yellow Medicine.

"My grandson, who will mend your moccasins? Who will cook for you?" she wailed, and threatened to roll off the pony drag and walk back if he made her go away.

"Little Grandmother, there is nothing for you to cook," explained Kaduza patiently.

One sleepless night in Winona's log lodge convinced Uncida that she could not and would not stay the winter. Her spirit, she told them all, could not bear to live in a lodge with corners. Her spirit could not live without a cheerful open fire inside the *tipi*. Her spirit would get sick and die without roundness and a bright fire in the center of the roundness.

"If my daughter can tell me one thing Wakantanka made that is not round or rounded, I will stay," she said.

Of course they could not, but to their amazement they did persuade Uncida to be vaccinated by Dr. Williamson against the white man's sickness that made hot dry skin, red spots, and

114

running bowels and finally killed. Dr. Williamson had already vaccinated 1000 Wahpetonwan and Sisseton Dakota against the sickness.

"Dr. Williamson may stick me if my grandson will also be stuck," said Uncida, who would submit to any queer thing if it would keep her well to take care of the grandson that was close to her.

Thus Kaduza once again saw John Williamson, who was about to return to college after helping his father finish building the mission school during his two-month vacation. John greeted him warmly with the white man's shaking-the-hand greeting.

"Ah, Inyanka Duza Tanka! Swift Runner! You are famous, you know! I wish I had been there to see that great run, but I was helping my father build his house."

After a brief visit with She Gathers Huckleberries and her son Taopi, who had joined the earnest and "all-the-way" Christian farmer Dakota, Kaduza and Uncida went back to their *tipi* in Little Crow's village on the Lower Reservation. Their parfleches had been flat when they left but now were fat with corn and potatoes, gifts from blood-relatives and *hunka*-relatives on the Upper Reservation. Being true Dakota, they shared their gifts with the have-nots in Little Crow's village. They shared, as well, all the news that they had gathered.

In the Moon of Snow Blindness the winter before, the mission at Lac qui Parle had burned to the ground. Renville's ancient Holy Book that spoke the French language had burned with it.

Missionary Riggs and his family had come to Yellow Medicine to build another mission in the nearby village of Yellow Medicine, and many of the Christians from Lac qui Parle had moved there to be with them.

On their way to collect their annuity payments, the Sisseton Dakota were causing much trouble to their Wahpetonwan brothers and sisters by stealing from their fields and their gardens—even from their *tipis* and log lodges if no one was home, and usually there was not, for everyone, even the very young and the very old, had to present themselves at their agency for the distributing of the money and provisions and the reckoning with the traders.

"When Tunkasida and I were young," sighed Uncida, "no Dakota ever went into a *tipi* that was closed and had two crossed sticks before it."

Even in the rare times when there was enough corn and potatoes, Uncida and the old ones sighed about the food. "Our stomachs are not satisfied with corn," they said. "Our stomachs ache with longing for the meat of buffalo, deer, bear, and fowl. Wakantanka made the Dakota stomach to eat meat. The Dakota stomach needs meat to keep strength in the body."

Kaduza did his best to get fish and muskrats for Uncida's iron pot, but with thousands of other Indians on the two reservations trying their best to do the same for their black pots, the muskrats and fish became more and more scarce.

Where were the cattle the white men had promised? Where was everything else the white men had promised? Where were the government schools that had been promised in the treaties? The only schools so far were the mission schools, and there was no mission school as yet on the Lower Reservation. Were the missionaries on the Upper Reservation getting the money that was supposed to go to the Dakota for schools? There were many tongues on the Lower Reservation that spread that rumor. Many ears heard it and many hearts believed it.

The ugliest rumors, however, were spread about the Dakota men who adopted white dress, cut their hair, and put their hands to the plow. By 1859 200 Dakota males had done so. In recognition of their willingness to travel the white man's road the agents on the two reservations gave them fields, wagons, oxen, tools, and houses. Soon some of them were living in one-and-a-half story brick houses 16 x 24 feet—the bricks made by the Dakota farmer's own hands.

"No need to ask where the money promised to us is going!" fumed the Dakota who clung stubbornly to the blanket and the old ways.

Some of the farmer Dakota near the missions at Yellow Medicine and Hazelwood went even further. Abandoning their own

116

tribal band, they formed a new one, adopted a constitution, called themselves the Hazelwood Republic, and elected their own governor-chief. Eighteen men signed the constitution, promising to honor, respect, and obey the one true God and to respect the government and to drop Dakota customs, to adopt white dress, and to improve their condition. They requested that white officials treat them as white men and issue them their annuities separately from the other bands.

"Did *you* sign, my father?" Kaduza asked Red Beaver fiercely the next time he saw him. "Are you a member of this new band? These men of the great Dakota nation that have chosen to be not-a-relative? We hear that She Gathers Huckleberries' son Taopi has signed. Did *you?*"

"Restrain your anger, my son," answered Red Beaver quietly. "No, I did not sign. But," he continued, his voicing rising, "when I see what is happening to Dakota young men who refuse to work and want the agents to feed them, my heart is not proud. They are neither farmers nor warriors, neither tame dogs nor true dogs. It is no wonder that the white farmers around the reservations call Dakota lazy and good-for-nothing."

"The time may come when we will all be warriors again," said Kaduza ominously, thinking of the Warrior Lodge some of the young men on the Lower Reservation were secretly planning.

"When that time comes, may my spirit be sitting far away," Red Beaver murmured.

"Sitting where, my father! Your spirit will not be allowed into the white man's heaven because you are Dakota. It will not be allowed to sit in the campcircle of the Dakotas in the spirit world because it will be not-a-relative."

"Let us hope, my son, that there is a campcircle in the spirit world for orphan spirits!" chuckled Red Beaver.

As the Dakota farms increased in number, so did the bad feeling between the Dakota the white people distinguished as "Blanket Indians" and those they called "Civilized Indians." On the Lower Reservation some Dakota who favored shedding the blanket were murdered. There were some mysterious deaths that aroused suspicions of poisoning.

"Dakota *wakan*-men do not need the juice of poison roots to make a man die," said Uncida. "They need only the *wakan* power."

In the spring of 1857 by the white man's count, the anger of all the Dakota on both reservations, whatever the fork of their minds, was united against the agents, the Governor Father in St. Paul, and the Great Father in Washington. In the Moon of Snow-melting Inkpaduta and his renegade band, mostly relatives, murdered about 40 white settlers near the Okoboji Lakes in northern Iowa, captured four white women, and vanished. The Long Knives from Fort Ridgely attempted to find and punish the outlaw band whose war axes were raised against everyone, red or white. But the Long Knives sank to their hips in the soggy snow, and Inkpaduta and his band sped to the refuge of the Pipestone Quarries, brutally murdering one of the captive women along the way.

The reservation Dakota, not even the Wahpekutes from whose band Inkpaduta had been banished, had no kind thoughts for Inkpaduta and his band. They bitterly resented that Inkpaduta, even though he had not been invited to the treaty making, came insolently to the first annuity payment and demanded that the Dakota share what they had received. The reservation Dakota were also angry with the Long Knives because they had let the outlaw band escape. But their anger at Inkpaduta and the Long Knives was nothing compared to their anger at the government officials who suddenly demanded that *they* find, capture, and punish the Inkpaduta band! Indeed, they were told, there would be no more distribution of moneys and provisions until this was done!

United in their disgust, Dakota who normally felt unfriendly to each other began talking together. Kaduza found himself listening to the grumblings of old Napesni, whom he had known as a boy at Lac qui Parle and was one of the few baptized Christian Dakota males on the Lower Reservation.

"The white men talk with forked tongues," said Napesni to Kaduza. "They tell us to give up going on the warpath, and now they tell us to take the warpath against Inkpaduta."

118

"They demand that we avenge wrongs to them and will not let us avenge wrongs to us," said Kaduza. "They would not let us avenge She Gathers Huckleberries' sister. They would not let us avenge the killing of a little Dakota girl last summer by six Ojibways."

"*A-i-i-i-!* Little Susan Rainbow! She was one of Aunt Jane's girls! I knew her well," said Napesni.

It was Napesni who came to tell Kaduza and Uncida the latest news from the Yellow Medicine Agency. He had just returned from a short visit to Yellow Medicine and brought messages from their family there that all was well with them in spite of everything. The Sissetons from the far end of the Upper Reservation, he reported, had begun arriving to receive their annuities and were told that there would be none until Inkpaduta was captured. Meanwhile a thousand and more Yankton Dakota from the western prairies and the western division of the Dakota had arrived to protest the sale of the land at Traverse des Sioux, claiming that what the Wahpetonwans and Sissetons had sold was theirs. Thousands of excited Dakota were roaming restlessly around Yellow Medicine. The Long Knives had come with their guns and cannon. A Sisseton Dakota stabbed a Long Knife. The Long Knives' major demanded that the Dakota be delivered up. It was done—sullenly and unwillingly. The prisoner escaped and in escaping was shot in the leg and was carried to the Sisseton camp near Missionary Williamson's house. Dr. Williamson was called to treat the wounds. Meanwhile the father of the escaped young man heard the false rumor that his son was dead and thought that Dr. Williamson had killed him. The Sisseton father entered the Williamson house through the back door, a gun hidden in his blanket. Dr. Williamson's sister Aunt Jane was cooking at the stove. She cheerily invited the Sisseton Dakota father to sit down and eat some food. Being very hungry, he did so and in the meantime learned that his son was not dead and that Dr. Williamson had treated his wounds.

"What a time of it we had!" exclaimed Napesni.

More bands of Dakota arrived at both agencies for the distribution of the annuities, adding to the thousands already wait-

119

ing. Children wailed with hunger, tempers shortened, tensions mounted.

Finally Little Crow offered to go seek out the Inkpaduta band. "A lawless man of another band has done wrong, and we are made to suffer for it. For this our women and children are starving!"

Kaduza was one of the 106 who volunteered to go with Little Crow.

"Is it to win an eagle feather at last, my grandson?" asked Uncida. "At last an eagle feather?"

"The son of Strong Heart would sooner count coup on a skunk than on Inkpaduta, son of Black Eagle, who murdered his own chief, The Cane. Inkpaduta, who murdered War Eagle That May Be Seen and his men as they slept in a hunting camp! No, my grandmother, it is not for glory we go. As you see, we do not paint, we do not dance."

Because there was no time to take Uncida to the Upper Reservation, Kaduza took her to Snana's house until his return. Uncida sang a brave-hearted song as they went along, but they did not say good-bye. They did not need to, for Uncida sent her thoughts along with her grandson and knew that he left his thoughts with her.

Little Crow and his men found Inkpaduta and his band to the north and west, close to Yankton territory. Two of their captives had been sold to Yankton Dakota and then ransomed by Little Paul and Other Day, Christian farmer Dakota near the Yellow Medicine Agency. Mrs. Noble had been handed over to the sons of Walking Spirit, a Christian chief at Lac qui Parle. The sons of Walking Spirit had come to the outlaw camp and boldly told Inkpaduta that he had done a shameful thing. Not so, Inkpaduta had responded. What he had done was a daring and extraordinary thing. Its very audacity made it a hero thing. Wait and see!

The two sons of Walking Spirit brought Mrs. Noble to their father's *tipi*, where the chief's wife treated her so lovingly that when her white rescuers came she at first refused to be rescued!

If Little Crow and his men had been on an avenging party,

they no doubt would have wiped out Inkpaduta's whole band. After killing three of them, Little Crow returned to the Lower Agency, announcing to all ears that they had done enough to avenge the wrong to the white men. Let the Long Knives do the rest! But by this time the Long Knives could not care less. Major Cullen, superintendent of Indian affairs in St. Paul, dropped the whole affair and finally ordered the annuities to be distributed—all of which only increased Little Crow's and every Dakota's bitterness and contempt and convinced them that the white men were as weak and faint-hearted as rabbits.

The next year brought an event that inflamed hatred toward the whites even more and increased tensions between the factions within the four Dakota bands on the two reservations. In the bitter cold of the Moon of the Raccoons, 26 chiefs and headmen of the four eastern bands of the great Dakota nation assembled at the Lower Agency. There they were joined by a large party of white men escorting them to Washington, D.C., by way of sleds to McGregor, Iowa, ferry to Prairie du Chien, and train from Prairie du Chien to Chicago and Washington.

Kaduza stood with a group of young men from Little Crow's village and watched the departing Dakota leaders and the white men climb into the sleighs and wrap themselves in buffalo robes. Agent Joseph Brown's horses already looked worn out from having been driven 430 miles from his home in Henderson, Minnesota, all over the Upper Reservation collecting the chiefs and headmen.

Kaduza knew some of the chiefs by sight and by asking learned who the others were. Among those from the Upper Reservation were Akepa, Scarlet Eagle Feather, Red Iron, Other Day, Little Paul, Iron Walker, Stumpy Horn, Sweet Corn, and Extended Tail Feathers. Among those from the Lower Reservation were Little Crow, Big Eagle, Traveling Hail, Red Legs, Mankata, Wabasha, and Has a War Club. Kaduza saw Dr. Thomas Williamson climbing into a sleigh and guessed that he was going along to take care of any who might become ill on the long journey. He recognized at least four traders and wondered why they were going along. Indeed, what was the purpose

121

of this large delegation going to Washington? He asked a Wah-pekute next to him, one of the militant braves who was saying that the young men had to take things into their own hands and organize a Warrior Lodge.

"Which purpose?" sneered the Wahpekute. "The one the white men spoke with their lips or the crooked óne they hid in their hearts?"

Someone else wondered why the Dakota chiefs were being taken to Washington. Why did not the white chiefs and headmen in Washington come to the reservation?

The Wahpekute had an answer for that, too. "To get our old men so far away from us that they cannot hear our voices raised against what the white men want them to do."

Five months and 3500 miles later—far too late to plant their corn—the delegation came back. Whatever awe they had felt at all they had seen and heard was drowned in their bitterness at what had happened to them in Washington. Perhaps there was fear in their hearts, too, at having to explain to their young men, their young hotbloods, what they had done. For they had all finally and reluctantly put their X's to a treaty selling one-half of their two reservations. All the land north of the Minnesota River—889,000 acres! And, as it finally turned out, for 30 cents an acre instead of the dollar an acre they had been led to expect.

Even Napesni's Christian Dakota blood boiled. "Our lands are getting smaller and smaller," he said to Kaduza. "Soon the Great Father in Washington will have to put his Red Children on wheels so that he can move them whenever and wherever he feels like it."

But Napesni did not go to the meetings that turned into shouting battles and where words were hurled like mud balls. After all the words had been thrown, Little Crow rose wearily and said, "What is the matter with you? Are your ears stopped up? How many times must I tell you that we did bring all these grievances to the ears of the Great Father in Washington. There is not one wrong you mention that we did not bring to his ears.

122

But our words were *worthless*. We could just as well have spoken them to the wind."

Little Crow was unable to explain to the hotbloods that the chiefs' resistance had gradually been worn down by the waiting and delaying tactics, by the dust, heat, and humidity of Washington, by the sheer boredom of life in a cheap hotel in a city, by the hopelessness of fighting the white man's greed, by the desperate hope that perhaps the white men would *finally* be satisfied. The Dakota had once hoped that the white men would not cross the Mississippi. Perhaps now they would be satisfied and not cross the Minnesota, and the Dakota nation could live west of the Minnesota as long as the rivers flow and the grasses grow.

Realizing that all the Wahpetonwan Dakota in his old home at Lac qui Parle now had to move across the river, Kaduza went on a month's journey to visit them. He left Uncida at her daughter's lodge near Yellow Medicine. This time Uncida did not protest. She closed her eyes to the square corners and was all eyes for Winona's babies. There were two now. A second baby girl had been born and had been baptized Nancy after Missionary Williamson's daughter Nancy Jane.

At Lac qui Parle Kaduza sought out Jean Baptiste Renville and found him to be changed and yet the same *koda*-friend. A friend who hid nothing in his heart from him and spoke the truth, even when the truth stung like a hornet.

After telling Kaduza that he planned to move down to Missionary Rigg's Hazelwood Mission to be with the Christian Dakota there, Jean Baptiste promptly spoke his troubled thought. "My friend, you have seen 26 winters, and yet you have not gone to school. My nephews and nieces, who have not seen seven winters yet, can read and write. You are a very intelligent man, my friend, but you do not show much intelligence when you refuse to learn to read and to write. I hear that the Episcopal church is planning to start a mission school at the Lower Agency. Why do you not go to it?"

"Perhaps you think too highly of reading and writing," answered Kaduza evenly. "Even more than the white people do.

123

White men do not seem to remember what is written on papers!"

"You have not changed at all, I see. You are still so intelligent there is no use arguing with you! So—let us not argue."

Kaduza and Uncida returned to Little Crow's village on the Lower Reservation for another long hard winter. Uncida never did quite learn how to cook with the provisions distributed by the agent. Hapanna and Winona had tried to teach her how to make bread from the white man's flour, but after one trial and taste Uncida said that white man's bread with all its holes looked too much like the lungs of an animal. "Lung bread is not for Dakota people," she said.

When the first young green showed on the cottonwood trees, Kaduza greeted it with a silent prayer of gratitude that Uncida had been strong enough to endure another cold and hungry winter. Uncida greeted the tender green leaves with one of her prayer songs, thankful that the grandson who was close to her had been strong enough to endure another cold and hungry winter.

But the summers now were often as hungry as the winters. What the agent distributed, complained the Dakota, was a little of everything and not enough of anything.

In October of 1860 Kaduza and some of his friends went into Yankton territory to hunt for buffalo. Once again he left Uncida with Snana, who loved having an old grandmother in her house.

When Kaduza returned toward the end of the Moon When the Deer Rut, he had enough buffalo meat to last through the Moon of Popping Trees—that is, until he had given away more than half of it to Snana and to the have-nots.

Although Kaduza had offered many times to do so, Uncida still refused to let him build the *tipi* fire. "My body would be ashamed to sit by a fire made by a man," she said.

"But times are changing, my grandmother. The axe is no longer a Dakota woman-tool. It has become a Dakota man-tool."

"Never in my *tipi!*" said Uncida.

But she let him go to the root cellar she and some of her friends had dug out to store potatoes and turnips from the cold.

124

She threw hurry words at him, for already her stomach was clamoring for the buffalo soup she was planning to make.

On the way back to Uncida's *tipi* with the potatoes and turnips, Kaduza met Napesni. His face was not only open and revealing. It glowed like the bark of the red willow in the spring.

"My friend," he announced simply, "John has come!"

17

Let Them Eat Grass!

So their roads came together again! Three times now. First at Lac qui Parle, where both of them had been born. And according to Uncida, a *wakan* thing had happened in the sky when each of them had been born. On the night of his own birth, the sky had rained stars. In the moon and year John was born a great *wakan* light had appeared in the sky. The second time their roads had come together was at Kaposia. And now once again at Redwood Agency on the Lower Reservation.

Hiya! Not just three times. Four! The sacred Dakota number. John had also appeared in his vision—the great bonfire dying to ugly ash, John and he himself acting out the *heyoka* ritual, John and he himself dancing the Sun Dance. Was the true meaning of that strange vision finally going to be unwrapped? But did he really want it unwrapped? Some mysteries were better left unwrapped, like a blight-eaten ear of corn. If the true meaning was meant to come, it would come. He would not flee from it, but neither would he run to meet it—or help it to come.

Thus Kaduza made John a person to be avoided, somebody whose eyes and presence one eluded. Yet in the next two years he knew almost as much about John Williamson as did Napesni, in whose *tipi* John lived and to whose *tipi* he invited the handful of Christian Dakota on the Lower Reservation to worship on the Holy Day. It was not even a handful of Christians, for some of

126

the Indians were already going to the Episcopal mission to worship. Among these were Snana and her husband.

Kaduza knew that John was seeking out every Dakota he had known at Lac qui Parle and Kaposia. When John finally scratched discreetly at the closed flap of Uncida's *tipi* one day in the Moon When the Deer Shed Their Horns, Kaduza welcomed him as politely as did Uncida. He showed him to the lean-back to his left, his heartside, the place of honor for a guest. Uncida sat on the left side of the *tipi* near the door, busily mending Kaduza's hunting moccasins and modestly guarding her eyes.

After a gentle silence, John began speaking in fluent Dakota. "My friend, I have been hoping that your swift feet would find the way to Napesni's *tipi*. We have many things to talk about, we two old friends."

"My friend, the feet know the way to Napesni's *tipi*, but the ears are unwilling to hear that our Dakota way is bad, that our Dakota life is bad, and that we must learn the ways of the white man and worship his god."

"But that is not what I teach and preach," said John quietly. "I teach Jesus Christ, who is the truth that is higher than all other truths."

"Your Jesus Christ may be the highest truth for your people, but he is not the highest truth for our people. All that you teach is no doubt true for your people, but not for our people. The Great Spirit made us different nations. The Great Spirit knows what is best."

"Our Father above sent his Son Jesus Christ for every nation on earth."

"If the Son of God ever crossed the Salt Water and found the red men, our Dakota nation never heard of it."

John turned on his lean-back and looked long and earnestly into Kaduza's face. A boyish smile lit his eyes before it touched his lips. "It is good to talk with you, Swift Runner. You speak straight. You speak from the heart. May your ears and your heart someday be ready and willing to hear about Jesus Christ. But let us talk of other things. My heart is troubled by the young men on the reservation. We hear rumors of their forming a Warrior Lodge."

"What do the white men want our young men to do? Shall we forget the glories of our fathers and become women? Shall we put on petticoats? Shall we sit in our mother's or grandmother's *tipis* and grow big bellies?"

"My fear is that the young men will create troubles and cause blood to be shed."

"My friend, we are not troublemakers. We are protectors of our people. Do you know who the real troublemakers are? The traders! The worst of all is that Myrick. Who will get all the money that is supposed to be paid for the land the four Dakota bands sold to the white men? The traders! Our young men want to be sure that those troublemakers and traders do not rob us of what is ours."

But after John had gone back to Napesni's *tipi*, Kaduza sat and stared into the fire until Uncida urged him to eat.

He had told John no lies, but had he kept back truths? And was that not lying? Were the young men on the reservation really *akicita*-protectors, keeping the Dakota disciplines more strictly than anyone else? Kaduza wished that he could forget all the times he had seen young Dakota braves playing cards with white men's cards and gambling away all their annuity money. Did they keep the rituals of their Dakota religion? Kaduza remembered his father facing the east every morning and singing a prayer of gratitude for the new day. Who felt grateful for anything any more? And who of his friends smoked the sacred pipe in the sacred way? They smoked—ho, how they smoked! But no longer did they smoke the sacred way or smoke the sweet kinnikinnik, the true Dakota tobacco.

Yes, they talked secretly of a Warrior Lodge. But did they know what it meant to be a Dakota warrior? They were hot-tempered. They talked a lot, boasted of what they were going to do. What was it his father had called him when he had done that as a man-boy? *Tankada!* Too Big for His Moccasins!

Kaduza's thoughts lingered with his dead father. "My father," he whispered, "be glad that you are in the Land of Spirits. We are fast ceasing to be what we were. My father, is there something your son can do? Is there something your son can do to help our great Dakota nation? Is there something your son can do to bring purpose and power to the young Dakota men crowded together on this reservation with no meaning and purpose for their lives?"

The Sun Dance! Tunkasida, his grandfather, had danced the Sun Dance when the hearts of his people were on the ground. So Uncida had told him. Was this what he could do to do the right thing for his people? Would watching him suffer the ordeal of the Sun Dance help his young restless and bitter friends find their true selves? Would it help him find his true self? If so, he would do it! That he would! And soon!

Kaduza raised his head. "My grandmother, how does a Dakota brave prepare to dance the Sun Dance?"

Uncida, whose greatest joy now was remembering her whole life, was startled from her remembering.

"Do my ears hear my grandson speak of the Sun Dance?"

"Tell me again, my grandmother, how my grandfather prepared to dance the Sun Dance."

Uncida's thoughts flew happily back again to their sweet remembering.

"Tunkasida purified his body by fasting. He cleansed his body in the sweat lodge. Tunkasida purified his heart by prayer. He cleansed his heart of all hatred, of all thoughts of revenge. Tunkasida told me that no one can dance the Sun Dance who carries hatred and revenge in his breast."

"Then who can dance the Sun Dance?" asked Kaduza bitterly. "No one that I know, and I least of all!"

In a kind of despair Kaduza shut his heart after that night to thoughts of right paths he might take to help his sick Dakota nation and opened his heart to thoughts of wrongs against the Dakota nation. Instead of brooding over the wrongs in solitude as he had done before, he joined other young men in reciting the wrongs to each other's ears. Indeed, the recitation of wrongs almost became a litany. The old warriors still sat cross-legged around *tipi* fires on winter nights and recited their brave deeds.

129

The young frustrated would-be warriors sat and recited their litany of injustices. The list lengthened, and so did the litany.

Cursed be the greedy white men who take and take and give so little.

Cursed be the Father in Washington who brought our Dakota chiefs to Washington and treated them like children and made them sell half our reservation.

Cursed be the chiefs for signing the papers.

Cursed be the traders who got all the money for the land.

Cursed be the white men who make farms and fences on our old hunting grounds and drive away the game.

Cursed be the missionaries who come among us to force their religion upon us, change our habits, make us work, and make us live like them.

Cursed be the Cut-hairs who betray their Dakota blood.

Cursed be the white men who have taken away our freedom to hunt and to camp where we choose.

Cursed be the Fathers at St. Paul who took away the old agents, who were bad, and sent us new ones, who are worse.

The last petition was added after the Republicans won the elections in 1861 and replaced all the Democrats in office with Republicans, even down to the white blacksmiths on the reservations. No matter how bad the old agents and officials were, they at least understood the Dakota and their ways better than the

130

new ones. A new agent, a new superintendent of the government schools that had finally been started, a new superintendent of farming, and a new blacksmith moved onto the Lower Reservation. The new agent was Thomas J. Galbraith, who was as arrogant as he was ignorant of the Dakota people. Kaduza and the other young Dakota braves immediately took a violent dislike to him. They added another petition to their litany.

Cursed be Galbraith, who treats us like children and thinks we have no thoughts in our heads.

In the Moon of Grass-greening, Kaduza and the young Dakota men seethed with excitement when white brothers went to war with white brothers. They gathered at the Redwood Agency almost daily to hear the latest news from the battle fronts. When they heard the number of casualties in the North's great defeat at Bull Run, they were staggered.

Kaduza's bitter joke traveled across the reservation and even reached Red Beaver's ears on the Upper Reservation. "White men go to war with their own brothers. Kill more men than we can count. White man's Great Spirit looks down and says, 'Good white men! Come to my home in the sky!' Dakota men go on warpath. Kill one Ojibway. White man's Great Spirit looks down from the sky and says, 'Bad Dakota! Go to the Bad Place and burn forever!' "

The bitter joke came to John Williamson's ears as well and brought him searching for Kaduza. He found him with a group of long-haired blanket Dakota lounging outside of Myrick's store, a long, narrow building with living quarters above. John's eyes quickly found Kaduza's face among the sullen, hostile, closed faces.

When Kaduza made no move to step out of the group and greet John, John spoke to him over the heads of the others. "Kaduza, my brother, what you have said about Our Father Above has come to my ears. My heart prays that it was only your mouth that spoke and not your heart. My heart prays that the cloud will be taken from your eyes and that you may see

131

the true face of the Father Above. He sent us his Son Jesus Christ to show us that true face. It is a suffering face. Our Father Above weeps for every man killed in battle, red or white. Kaduza, Our Father Above weeps!"

"If the white Father Above weeps, then an ocean of tears should be falling from the sky for all the Long Knives being killed in their war!" jeered one of the young Dakotas. "I raise my hands to the sky and feel no wetness!"

A shout of taunts and jeers went up. With a long, sad look at Kaduza, John turned and walked away.

"*Inina!* Be still!" Kaduza's harsh command silenced the jeers. He swiftly separated himself from the group and overtook John. Reaching out his hand in the white man's way of greeting, he said, "My brother, you speak straight. You do not hide what is in your heart. You do not lie. You have not come to take from us. You have come to give from your heart to us. My heart is as bitter as a gourd against the white man, but it has no bitterness in it for you."

Before John could reply, Kaduza swiftly loped away and did not return that day to his friends.

In the autumn of 1861 the new Republican officials in the Bureau of Indian Affairs at St. Paul, hoping to do away with the Dakota Sioux's hostility, issued a long-promised gift of money, an extra bonus that when it came amounted to $2.50 a head! However, the money was taken from the funds for the next summer's annuity payment! In the chaos and confusion of a country waging a civil war, Congress was slow about restoring the annuity fund. Because of the crop failure in the summer of 1862, the Dakota were already hungry, hungrier than ever before. They were reduced that summer to a diet of wild roots. But where on the prairie were there roots enough for the thousands of Dakota who began arriving in June for their annuity payments—payments that did not arrive until it was too late.

Early on Wednesday morning, August 13, 1862, Kaduza left Uncida, an Uncida with deep furrows in her cheeks and bloodshot eyes, on her bed in the *tipi*.

132

"My body is very tired," she said, excusing her staying in bed, "but," she added cheerfully, "my thoughts are hard at work."

Kaduza rode to the Redwood Agency to join a council meeting Little Crow had called between the white men at the agency and the Dakotas of the Lower Reservation. He galloped past the four stores at the agency, stores that were stocked with food in anticipation of the coming payment but that the traders refused to issue on credit. Hundreds of Dakota were already at the agency. Being a member of the secret Warrior Lodge, Kaduza moved to the front of the crowd. Facing Little Crow and the Dakota were Agent Thomas J. Galbraith, the traders from the four stores, and other employees. An official interpreter was present to translate the deliberations. The only other white person present who knew both languages was John Williamson.

Little Crow stepped forward to speak. Because he had been one of the chiefs who had signed away half of the reservation, he had lost his role as chief spokesman for the eastern Dakota to his rival, Traveling Hail, who had opposed the sale of the land. But today Little Crow was the spokesman. The row of white men facing him did not understand what he said, but they heard and understood his passion. "We have waited a long time. The money is ours, but we cannot get it. We have no food, but here are these stores filled with food. We ask that you, the agent, make some arrangement by which we can get food from the stores, or else we may take our own way to keep ourselves from starving. When men are hungry they help themselves."

The official interpreter quailed before the threat in Little Crow's speech and refused to translate it.

"Williamson," said Agent Galbraith sharply, "what did Little Crow say?"

In a clear, level, and neutral voice John Williamson translated Little Crow's speech.

Agent Galbraith turned to the four storekeepers. "Well, boys, it's up to you now. What do you plan to do?"

The four men stepped aside and talked in low tones, took their seats again and said nothing. The Dakota waited silently. The agent grew impatient. "Well, boys, speak up! What is it to be?"

133

"Whatever Myrick does we will do," said one of them. "We are not proprietors, anyway."

"Well, Myrick?" the agent asked.

Without a word Myrick rose and started to leave.

"Look here, Myrick, you have got to say what you will do!"

Slowly and deliberately the trader Myrick turned and faced the Dakota. "If they are hungry, let them eat grass! As for me, I don't give a damn!"

Kaduza, understanding not a word of any of this, kept his eyes on John Williamson's face. He saw the swift startled look of disbelief. The official interpreter turned as white as a white man can get.

"What did he say? What did he say?" cried the Dakota.

The official interpreter was too shaken to interpret.

"Well, Williamson, I guess we will have to depend on you again," said Agent Galbraith.

For one brief second John Williamson's eyes met Kaduza's, and Kaduza felt as if he were looking through them into a darkly suffering heart. Then loudly, clearly, John Williamson translated trader Myrick's words into Dakota. "*Docinpi hecin, deji yutwicasi po!*"

There was a moment of dead silence. Then with wild cries and war whoops the Dakota raced away to Little Crow's village. Kaduza was swept along with them.

18

What I Have Done, I Have Done

Long before morning stood up the following Monday Kaduza rattled the flap covering Napesni's *tipi* and called softly but urgently. When Napesni thrust his head through the door and asked sleepily who was there, Kaduza whispered, "If you are John's friend, you must persuade him to go away at once. His life is in danger."

"John left yesterday for Ohio," said Napesni. "Who can have evil thoughts in his heart to kill John?"

"There are thoughts in many hearts to kill all whites. John is white. It is good that he has gone."

Uncida had just fallen asleep after lying awake waiting for Kaduza until the night was very old.

Kaduza shook her gently. "Rise up, my grandmother. You must fly away at once to your daughter. Come, Fleet-of-foot is waiting."

"The Hahatonwan?" asked Uncida, scrambling from her buffalo robe and seizing an axe. "I am not afraid! I will kill the enemy!"

Over Uncida's protests, Kaduza lifted her onto Fleet-of-foot. This time Uncida did not ride the pony drag but rode in Kaduza's arms, rode as swiftly as she had ever ridden. Indeed, Kaduza rode as if they were being pursued. But should a Dakota warrior be running *away from* the enemy, carrying an old grandmother in his arms? Uncida peered up at Kaduza's face, but the stern set of his jaws forbade any questions. Not that Kaduza did not have similar thoughts running in circles about what he was doing and pointing accusing fingers at it.

"This is war!" Little Crow had said but two hours ago when aroused from sleep by his wildly excited young men and told of the killing of three white men and two white women by four Mdewakantonwan young men returning from a hunt in the Big Woods.

"This is war!" Little Crow had said. "White blood has been shed. White women have been killed. The Long Knives will take terrible vengeance."

War had been declared, and he, Kaduza, a Dakota warrior and a member of the Warrior Lodge, was galloping away from the planned attack on the agency, an attack that was taking place right now. And why was he galloping away? To carry an old woman to safety!

But other thoughts turned and faced the accusing, shaming thoughts. Had not his heart this early morning clearly told him to pick up this frail little grandmother and take her to safety? And did not his heart tell him that this was the right thing to do? Once she was safe with Hapanna and Red Beaver, he would return and join the battle. *Hoka!* The Dakota nation would unite to drive the white men back behind the Mississippi! Who knows? The Winnebagos might join them! Ah, perhaps even the Ojibway! Did not they, too, want their country back again and their freedom to roam and to hunt?

Hapanna was surprised and overjoyed to see Uncida but grieved to see her sunken cheeks and promptly began cooking a soup from the rabbit Red Beaver had shot higher up on the Yellow Medicine River. Red Beaver was equally surprised and overjoyed, but knowing that Uncida clung to the old ways, he promptly left with Kaduza to rub down Fleet-of-foot and stake her at the grazing place. Red Beaver waited silently for Kaduza to tell him the reason for this unexpected visit.

"Until yesterday the Mdewakantonwan and Wahpekute young men only dreamed and boasted of going on the warpath against the white men," Kaduza said.

136

"Our ears have heard rumors of this."

"Yesterday four young men of Shakopee's band—Brown Wing, Breaking Up, Killing Ghost, and Runs Against Something When Crawling—killed three white men and two white women. They were returning from a hunt across the Minnesota and up near the Big Woods."

"They were fools!"

"They were hungry. They were starving. We are all starving down on the Lower Reservation! They were coming empty-handed from the hunt and found a nest of eggs near the white farmer's fence. One took them up to eat. The others warned him about troubles with the white man. They quarreled. 'You are a coward!' 'I am not a coward. I am not afraid of the white man!' 'Prove it!' 'Watch me, then! I will go to the white man's house and shoot him!' That is how it started."

"And how will it end?" Red Beaver asked.

"We shall drive the white man back across the Mississippi. Most of the white men have gone to be soldiers in the white man's war. So many have already been killed that the Long Knives come from St. Paul asking for half-breed Indians to come and help them fight their war. The white men are weak. Now is the time to win back the land that belongs to the Dakota nation!"

"Fools! Fools!" groaned Red Beaver. "You will die like buffalo. You will kill ten white men and ten times ten will come to kill you."

"So said Little Crow to us early this morning."

"Little Crow, then, consents to lead you fools on the war-path?"

"Little Crow calls us fools but says he is no coward and will die with us. Even now they are fighting and killing white men at Redwood."

Red Beaver looked keenly at Kaduza. "Will they not miss you? My son, why did you come here today? Will they not call you a coward?"

"As soon as Fleet-of-foot has rested I will return."

Kaduza stroked Fleet-of-foot behind the ears. At last he raised

137

his eyes to meet Red Beaver's. "It was to bring Uncida to safety. It was to warn you and my mother and sister and all the Christian Dakota that their lives are in danger. Your life, my father, and the lives of all the other Cut-hairs are in danger. It was to warn the missionaries that they will be killed if they do not flee. You must go at once to tell Missionary Williamson and Missionary Riggs to leave at once. If this is being untrue to my Dakota nation," he said bitterly, "then I am untrue."

"My son!" Red Beaver came swiftly around the horse's head and put his hand on Kaduza's shoulder. "Your anger is strong. It is strong enough to kill. Yet you think of the living. It is a braver thing to protect the living than to take life."

"My dead father always told me it is a brave thing to kill an enemy, and the white men are enemies of the Dakota nation."

"Perhaps it is a braver thing to make an enemy a friend."

Kaduza looked steadily at Red Beaver. "How can day and night be friends? How can two men be friends if one of them thinks himself higher than the other? The white men scorn us. They treat us as if we were rotten fish. You, my father, should know that the Dakota and the white men can never be friends. What happened to the Hazelwood Republic? Why did it fail? Because the white men scorn the Dakota even when they leave the road of their fathers and walk the white man's road. All of those who signed the Hazelwood Republic papers promised to live the white man's way. But when they went to Mankato and asked to become citizens and to be treated as white men, as equals, the judge said, 'No, this cannot be. You do not speak or write English.' Other Day told the judge that they all spoke and wrote the Dakota language. And what did the judge in Mankato say, my father? 'The Dakota language is no language. It has no literature!' And what did he mean by that, my father? He meant that we are not a people, we are not a nation. For them we will never be a people and a nation!"

"What you say is true, my son, but the path the Mdewakantonwans and the Wahpekutes are taking is not the path to convince the white men that we are their equals. It will only make them all the more sure that we are what they think we are, wild

138

savages. You must not expect the Wahpetonwans and the Sissetons to join you in this madness."

"My father, when the Wahpetonwans and Sissetons see the
Long Knives fleeing from the Mdewakantonwans and the Wahpekutes, they will come like wild geese to the rice fields. Like it
or not, my father," said Kaduza with a grim smile, "I go to kill
white men, as many white men as I can kill."

Kaduza mounted Fleet-of-foot and rode an arrow's flight toward the south before he turned his horse and came back. "My
father," he said earnestly, "take care of my grandmother and
mother and sister. And of yourself, my father, take care of yourself and go at once to warn the missionaries to flee."

"My son," said Red Beaver, "you speak and act from a divided
heart."

"At least it is not half-Dakota and half-white," said Kaduza,
turning southward again.

The trail between the Yellow Medicine Agency and the Redwood Agency, which had been so empty of travelers in the early
morning, was now lively with runners and men on horseback—
some going north, some south. Kaduza realized that they were
speeding with messages. All the Dakota villages scattered along
the river were being told of what had happened at the Redwood Agency and were being summoned to war. Very soon, he
was sure, the road would be thick with warriors from the Upper
Reservation riding to join their Dakota brothers in the attack on
Fort Ridgely. Once the fort was destroyed, the door would be
wide open to the whole great valley of the Minnesota and they
could drive the white men back across the Mississippi!

When Fleet-of-foot stumbled, Kaduza suddenly realized that
both she and he were at the point of collapse. If they forced
themselves to go on, they would both be no good for anything
by the time they reached Little Crow's village on the Lower
Reservation. He guided the horse off the trail into the tall prairie
grass, dismounted at the fringe of woods along the river, and led
the horse through to a small island of meadow on the shore
where Fleet-of-foot could drink or graze or rest. He staked the

139

horse, threw his blanket on the ground under a cottonwood, and was asleep before Fleet-of-foot could crop three mouthfuls.

Thus it was that Kaduza missed the events of that Monday when Little Crow's warriors attacked the Redwood Agency and killed 20 white people. The very first one to die was the storekeeper Myrick, whose mouth was stuffed with grass. Kaduza also missed the ambush of 46 Fort Ridgely soldiers under Captain John S. March at the Redwood Ferry. Twenty-four were killed, and the captain drowned while trying to escape by swimming across the river. Kaduza also missed the first violent wave of murdering the pioneer families now homesteading throughout the whole valley north of the Minnesota. If he had been awake that night, he would have seen the fires of many a building and haystack lighting the sky.

When Kaduza awoke at dawn, his hunger was so urgent that he waded and swam across the river and rode Fleet-of-foot in search of a white settler's farm where he might steal a few ears of corn. He soon came upon the still-smoldering ashes of a homestead. Near the root cellar, as if they had sought to hide there and had been dragged out, he found the naked, mutilated, and scalped bodies of the farmer, his wife, and infant daughter. So the Dakota warriors of the Lower Reservation had already ranged this far! Already they were clearing the Minnesota valley of the whites, and he, Kaduza, had not even begun to fight. By this time his brother-warriors must be attacking Fort Ridgely. Kicking Fleet-of-foot into a gallop, Kaduza turned her head southward.

Slowed by a copse of hazel brush and a creek crossing the farm, he suddenly spied two human forms in the thicket. He wheeled Fleet-of-foot around, dismounted, and parted the bushes. A white boy of about eight winters lay sleeping, his arm around a little girl. Their faces were streaked with dirt and tears and looked as if the wild nightmares of terror were galloping about in their heads. How these two had escaped the Dakota attack Kaduza did not know. Should he leave them sleeping and ride on? But they would only awaken and wander and meet other war parties and be killed. There was nothing to do but wake them up and take them back to Uncida and Hapanna.

Before he gently woke them, Kaduza did a strange thing even he could not understand. He rode back to the homestead, dragged the two bodies of the farmer and his wife side by side, and placed the infant with the crushed head in its mother's arms. He drove off the flies that had already begun to buzz around the bodies and covered the three with his blanket.

When the two children were awakened from their sleep of exhaustion and saw Kaduza's face, they were too terrified to scream. The boy sat up, clutched his sister tightly to himself, and looked half-defiantly, half-pleadingly at Kaduza. Kaduza stroked their heads gently until they seemed to understand that he had no wish to harm them. Placing them in front of him, Kaduza rode at an easy canter to the river. He dismounted and by washing his own face and drinking encouraged them to do the same. Then, as he had seen both his fathers do many times to his mother, he combed the little girl's tangled hair and braided it into two neat braids. The boy looked on wonderingly and said words to his sister that Kaduza knew were not the English language.

Once again Kaduza waded and swam the Minnesota River, the children high and dry on Fleet-of-foot's back. Avoiding the trail to the Yellow Medicine Agency and staying within the cover of the tall prairie grass, he made his way back to Hapanna's log lodge. Without asking a single question, Hapanna and Uncida took the white children into their arms. Something in Uncida's brown leathery wrinkled face made the little girl put her arms around her neck and cry softly. Uncida rocked her in her arms. "*Ay-e-e-e-e! Ay-e-e-e-e!* My little orphan. My pitiful one! I will be grandmother to you!"

Convinced that the white children were safe, Kaduza turned Fleet-of-foot southward once again, but before he was out of sight of Hapanna's lodge, he met Red Beaver riding at full and furious gallop from the Yellow Medicine Agency. Recognizing Kaduza, he pulled his horse to a rearing stop. Both his look and his silence were eloquent with rage. His horse champed the bit

141

and chafed at the tight rein. "My son, I come from a council meeting," said Red Beaver. "The Wahpetonwan refuse to join the Mdewakantonwan and Wahpekute in their madness!"

"So the old warriors—or should I say the old women—have voted not to join us!" Kaduza said with scorn. "But your young warriors have the honorable Dakota privilege to choose or change leaders. They will join us when they see us chasing the white men into the rising sun."

"It is the Dakota nation that will be scattered into the setting sun like autumn leaves before the wind," said Red Beaver. "My son, my heart is sick and sad from what we hear. You are murderers, thieves, butchers of women and children."

"Time will tell whose deeds are darker," said Kaduza coldly, kicking Fleet-of-foot in the ribs.

The sun had passed the middle of the sky and was traveling into gathering rain clouds when Red Beaver, who meanwhile had gone to Hapanna's lodge and seen the white children, overtook him.

"My son, you make me glad. You have restrained your anger and rescued two white children."

"What I have done, I have done," said Kaduza coldly. "Now I will restrain my anger no longer. I will take my anger to the place of battle. And this time I do not return!" he shouted back and galloped down the trail toward the Redwood Agency.

19

I Killed! I Killed!

The rain had started by the time Kaduza returned to Little Crow's village early in the evening. It was not a brief and violent thunderstorm but a steady rain that kept on all that night and most of the next day. Kaduza found the village in confusion, full of 400 Dakota warriors who had fought for five hours at Fort Ridgely but had been kept in the ravines by the cannon fire. Two hundred and more Dakota who had chosen to range the prairie to kill and to loot were returning with their scalps and loot and were telling of their feats. Children dressed themselves in the white men's breeches and white women's calico dresses and bonnets brought back by the raiders and play-acted the stories being told. Women were busy at cooking fires preparing meals for their husbands and brothers and sons from the swine, steer, and sheep caught and butchered on the raiding parties. Old women were running bullets and old men were cleaning guns for the next day's battle.

No one asked Kaduza where he had been these three days. Probably, he thought, because the raiders supposed that he had been in the attack on the fort, and the attackers on the fort supposed that he had been with the raiders—or else it was simply because it was Dakota courtesy not to ask curious and personal questions. When a brother in the secret Warrior Lodge he had joined asked him to eat at his fire, Kaduza discovered how famished he was.

As they ate, his Warrior Lodge brother told him how at first the Long Knives' chief at the fort had lined his soldiers up in the stupid Long Knives' way—everyone in straight lines and columns, all out in the open field, as if they were saying: "Here we are! As plain to see as a flock of pigeons on a dead tree on the open prairie. Shoot us down! Column by column!"

"The Long Knives soon dived behind their buildings and woodpiles," he chuckled, then added soberly, "It was their cannon that drove us back. Little Crow says that we can take the fort with more warriors. We return tomorrow. Do you come with us?"

"*Ho*," said Kaduza.

Because he was a swift runner and could creep through prairie grass and slip through thickets as silently as a fox, Kaduza was assigned to be a scout in the second attack on Fort Ridgely. The fort stood high on a plateau above the Minnesota and was surrounded by several wooded ravines, some of them several miles long. Any band of Long Knives coming to help those trapped in the fort would move toward the fort under cover of the ravines. If the scouts on night watch saw or heard anything alarming, they were to give the call of the screech owl, the night bird that gave the shivering cry. If there was nothing to give cause for alarm, the scouts were to give the nighthawk's cry.

So it was that Kaduza was actively engaged in the second attack on Fort Ridgely and did not kill a single white man. This time Little Crow had assembled 800 warriors—most of them Mdewakantonwans and Wahpekutes, some of them Wahpetonwans and Sissetons, a sprinkling of them Winnebagos. Attacking from the ravines to the northeast and the southwest, Little Crow's warriors took the stables and the sutler's store. But cannon fire aimed at the stables set the hay on fire, and the flames drove the Dakota back. Ducking the bullets from the ravines, two Long Knives grabbed a wounded Dakota and hurled him into the flames. Little Crow's attempt to join his forces from the two ravines was frustrated by cannon fire. All this Kaduza heard at a distance. Not knowing that only five cannon were involved and hearing the loud *boom-booms* echoing up and down the

144

valley, he thought that as many as ten times the fingers on his two hands were shooting.

But in all this Kaduza had no warrior part. His part was to scout and to see that no other Long Knives, no other big guns came to the relief of the fort. Camouflaged with prairie grasses, he probed every ravine to its end, scanned the prairies in every direction, scrutinized every boat or canoe that moved along the river. He ranged as far north as the old grown-over trail that crossed the creek flowing into the Minnesota from the north.

It was there that he crept close to a party of white people that had been approaching the fort on the old Lac qui Parle road but stopped before he gave the alarm. Now they were hiding in the underbrush and waiting. Kaduza recognized Missionaries Williamson and Riggs and their families and Aunt Jane. The others in the group he did not recognize, but all were white. Crouching in the willows, Kaduza was so close to them that he could see the weariness etched on their faces and hear their hushed voices. A child whimpered, and Kaduza saw Aunt Jane take it into her arms. He saw Dr. Williamson's son-in-law, Andrew Hunter, join the group and the others eagerly gather around him. He could not, of course, understand what was being said, but by the gestures and downcast looks he guessed that the son-in-law had crept to the fort to ask for protection and had been told that there were too many refugees there already, that it would be safer for them to go on. Two of the women broke into sobs but were hushed by the other women.

Dr. Williamson motioned the wives and children to climb into the wagon and buggy. He and Missionary Riggs grasped the bridles of the horses, led them across the creek and started off in a north-by-east direction. Kaduza followed them until they came out of the brush onto the prairie. Now was the time to give the screech owl signal; otherwise the party of whites would escape under cover of the gathering darkness. His warrior brothers, who had fought from midday until sundown, were in an ugly mood at having failed to take the fort and open the door to the valley. A call would bring them, thirsting for blood.

145

They would take out all their anger and frustration on this party of whites, sparing no one, not even the women and children.

Suddenly a whippoorwill called behind him and down the ravine from the direction of the Dakota encampment. It was the scouts' asking signal: "There is something suspicious. Is all well there where you are?"

Kaduza turned his head in the direction of the signal and gave an answering call. It was the cry of the nighthawk. "All is well!"

When morning got up, a large band of Dakota went down the river to New Ulm to attack it for the second time. Little Crow and another strong band went in the direction of the Big Woods. Once again Kaduza went with neither war party but was assigned to shadow the Dakota's old friend, the Long Trader Henry Sibley, who was on his way from Fort Snelling commanding an army of Minnesota volunteers to put down the Indian uprising. Kaduza and several other scouts were to spy on every move they made and report to Little Crow and the sub-chiefs wherever they were.

So once again Kaduza, who soon would be 29 winters and as yet had not killed an enemy and won the right to wear an eagle feather, was sent out as a scout and not a warrior. Fleet-of-foot carried him swiftly across the prairie between the Big Bend of the river to the town near Traverse des Sioux that the white men called St. Peter. He guided Fleet-of-foot around stray parties of Dakota raiders and remembered Little Crow's bitter remark that had the Mdewakantonwans and the Wahpekutes been more interested in going to war on the whites as a Dakota nation than in going on little killing and looting parties, by now they could have taken Fort Ridgely and New Ulm. And if they had had these victories to show, the Wahpetonwans and the Sissetons would have joined their effort to chase the white men back across the Mississippi forever. Kaduza rode past bodies lying where they had fallen, the ruin of homesteads, herds of untended cattle, cows bawling to be milked. Hiding Fleet-of-foot in a fringe of woods below St. Peter, Kaduza, keeping to gullies and low places, proceeded on foot, sometimes slithering through the tall grass on his stomach. Nothing escaped his eagle eyes, nothing of the chaos and confusion in the little town that suddenly had to house and feed hundreds of refugees flocking in from the valley as well as the citizen army of volunteers coming from all over the state to join the Long Trader's army of military troops.

By Monday, August 25, the forces numbered—so Kaduza thought—about 1400 men. That they were not well-supplied with ammunition he was able to gather from the sight of teapots and lead pipe being melted into bullets. Returning to Fleet-of-foot, Kaduza streaked across the prairie to report to Little Crow that the Long Trader was taking most of his troops to Fort Ridgely, but that Joseph R. Brown was leading about 150 men up the valley to find survivors and to bury the dead. Having made his report, Kaduza was sent to shadow Brown's men. From his places of hiding he watched them bury the bodies along the agency road, the bodies of Captain Marsh's men near the Redwood Ferry. He watched the men make camp across the river from the agency, near Birch Coulee, parking their wagons in a circle and picketing the cavalry horses.

All this Kaduza reported to the chiefs Big Eagle, Red Legs, Gray Bird, and Mankato, for Little Crow and his war party of 200 warriors were still skirmishing near the Big Woods. When he had emptied himself of his facts to the chiefs, he was told to ride to Fort Ridgely and shadow the Long Trader, who might come to the aid of Brown's men at Birch Coulee when the Dakota warriors attacked their encampment at dawn.

Trailing the Long Trader and his men marching from Fort Ridgely to the aid of Brown's men now circled and trapped at Birch Coulee was an easy but frustrating task. Easy because the Long Trader moved so slowly and stopped so long when he called a halt. Frustrating because the Dakota chiefs did not use the long delay to unite and charge on Brown's men pinned behind the 87 bodies of their dead horses. The Dakota braves were content to fight when they felt like it and then return to eat the hot meals their women, who had crossed the river, were preparing for them. Not until it was too late did they heed the faithfully reported information about the slow approach of the Long Trader's relief party.

"Cowards!" muttered Kaduza as he watched from a distance the Dakota warriors fall back and the Long Trader advance into the bullet-riddled encampment and shake hands with the survivors. In his blind anger at his Dakota brothers Kaduza drummed Fleet-of-foot's ribs and, paying no attention to directions, goaded her into a furious gallop. By the time he reached Beaver Creek, his anger had simmered down to disgust and he recognized where he was. Weary from his constant traveling these days and nights, he decided to return to Uncida at Yellow Medicine. Then, too, Little Crow's band and the other bands from the Lower Reservation had set up their villages there.

Kaduza turned Fleet-of-foot's head toward the west and rode into a settler's cornfield. It was while stooping to pluck an ear of corn to eat that he saw the white man and white woman crouching and cowering in the middle of the cornfield. Swiftly obeying his instincts, Kaduza's left hand grabbed the man's black beard and pulled him up onto his feet while his right hand seized his knife and raised it to strike. He felt a strange new power, the power to kill, surging up in him. At last, a white man to kill, to scalp, to show proof of his courage! Little Crow had made him a scout and not a warrior. Yet a scout is not someone who will not fight or kill. Now was his chance. Nothing to stop him now!

As swiftly as Kaduza raised his knife, the woman rose to her feet and clasped her hands around his left wrist. To Kaduza's surprise, she did not tear and claw at his hand but touched it pleadingly. At the same time the man's arms circled the woman's waist and tried to lift her away from himself and the poised knife. The power to kill suddenly drained away. Kaduza's left hand loosened its grip on the man's beard and his right hand clasping the knife dropped to his side.

He raised it again, but only to point to the east. By gestures and signs he attempted to tell the two to find the trail leading northeast to the Big Woods, to travel only at night, and to hide in the daytime. With that, he abruptly rode on, emerged from

148

the cornfield, and found himself near the still-smoking ashes of a homestead—the homestead of the two hiding in the cornfield, no doubt. A cow with two arrows stuck deep in her side was lying among the cabbages in the garden. When she saw Kaduza, she staggered to her feet and attempted to run away. Kaduza watched her pitiful efforts for a minute and then, leaping to the ground, thrust his knife deep into her heart. As the cow sagged to the ground, he pulled out the knife, held it up, dripping with blood, and looked at it intently.

Suddenly he laughed aloud, a shout of laughter that must have reached the two hiding in the cornfield. "I killed! I killed! Hear me, Four Winds! Kaduza with the bear heart, Kaduza has killed!"

Grabbing the cow's matted tail, he cut it off with a stroke. "I killed! I killed! Hear me, Four Winds, the brave Dakota warrior who is called Kaduza has gotten himself a scalp!" Still laughing, Kaduza tied the cow's tail to Fleet-of-foot's mane and rode toward the Minnesota River.

20

So This Is What It Is
to Be a Christian!

Kaduza was startled at the changes that had taken place in
so short a time at the Yellow Medicine Agency. His ears had
heard that the government buildings had been burned, but his
heart had not yet received the news. Now that his eyes saw ashes
where log buildings had stood and the huge stone walls of the
gutted warehouses, his heart, too, perceived. His eyes also saw
and his heart perceived the great sea of *tipis* that extended up
both the Minnesota and the Yellow Medicine Rivers. It seemed
as if all the Dakota from the Lower Reservation had moved up
to the Yellow Medicine.

But Kaduza was more amused than startled to see how many
Cut-hairs had gone back to the blanket. Some, indeed, had painted themselves. He could not resist taunting a Kaposian who had
been wearing pantaloons for years and now walked about in a
breechclout, his naked body streaked and stippled with paint.
"Too bad you cannot cover your cut hair with false hair!"

But Red Beaver, still wearing his farmer clothes with cool
dignity, was quite the same as before, and so was life within the
four walls of Hapanna's log lodge. If outside the great circle
of the sky was figuratively falling, if the Dakota *hunka* way of
life was literally being lost forever, Uncida and Hapanna seemed
not to know it. Fears and anxieties could not find room in their
hearts, for they were too busy taking care of the two white
orphans Kaduza had brought them. As for the children, Kaduza

150

scarcely recognized them in their Dakota clothes. Moreover, Uncida and Hapanna had transformed their white skin into red skin by a mixture of bear grease and paint. The little girl's red leggings were hung with ribbons, and the children's moccasins were brightly trimmed with quills and beads. Both the girl and the boy looked as happy and content as if they had been born to this way of life.

"Do you remember Snana, my grandson?" asked Uncida, who was braiding a bright ribbon into the little girl's hair. "When the last old moon died, Snana's little girl went to the Land of Spirits, and Snana's heart lay on the ground. But her brother brought her a white woman-child, and now Snana has a daughter again."

Having braided the little girl's hair, Uncida ran to fetch She Gathers Huckleberries, her old friend from Kaposia days. She, who had boasted so much of her sons, must hear that her grandson had returned from the battles. She must come and hear her grandson's battle stories!

Uncida and She Gathers Huckleberries sat on the dirt floor and feasted their eyes on Kaduza as he feasted on Hapanna's potato and turnip soup.

When he had finished, Uncida leaned eagerly toward him. "My grandson, did you make glory and gladness for yourself?"

"Little Grandmother, I made glory and gladness for myself."

"Do you have a scalp, my grandson?"

"Little Grandmother, my scalping knife is red with blood," said Kaduza solemnly.

The two old grandmothers waited patiently for the battle stories. When they did not come, Uncida sighed deeply. "My grandson is just like his grandfather. He will not boast of his glorious deeds!"

Kaduza's disillusion with the conduct of the war to drive the white men back across the Mississippi (or was it his disillusion with himself?) kept him from joining Little Crow's men, whom the Long Knives now called the Hostiles, for several days. But living among the Dakota who were called the Friendlies did nothing to ease the conflicts within him. Two events finally drove

151

him back into the camp of the Hostiles to join their last desperate attempt to win a victory.

The first was his meeting with Jean Baptiste Renville and their long talk together in which they, as of old, hid nothing in their hearts. That his *koda*-brother Jean Baptiste had continued his education in the white man's schools and that he had married a white wife—this Kaduza had already heard. But to his astonishment he discovered him living nearby as a—if not a prisoner, at least a carefully watched too-friendly-with-the-whites half-breed. Red Beaver told him that Jean Baptiste could have made himself great glory with the whites if he had done as Other Day had done and led a large party of whites to safety. But he had chosen instead to stay and do what he could to keep his brother Wahpetonwans from joining the Lower Reservation Dakota in their desperate and despairing attack on the whites.

By arrangements made through Red Beaver the two *koda*-friends met and rode up the Yellow Medicine River until they were out of sight of houses and *tipis*. It was a beautiful fall day, the kind of a fall day the Dakota called "a gopher's last look back." The young men dismounted, let their horses graze, and dropped down the bluff to the bank of the river, where there was nothing but themselves and the flowing water.

Jean Baptiste was the first to break the long silence. "My brother, why are you making war on the white men?"

"My brother," answered Kaduza, "why are you *not* making war on the white men? Perhaps," he added thoughtfully, "perhaps it is because you are married to a white woman. You love her and will not give her pain. If I loved a white woman, perhaps I would feel the same way."

"I love my wife, but she is not the reason I am not making war on the white men. My reason is Jesus Christ. He is my brother. He says all men are brothers."

"Never!" said Kaduza vehemently. "Agent Galbraith my brother? Trader Myrick my brother? Are you blind, my friend? Do you not see how they cheat, steal, and drive us ever westward? Is that what learning to talk and read and write like a white gentleman does to a Dakota man? Makes him blind? Is that what

152

learning to name all the books of the white man's Holy Book and to sing all the missionaries' songs does? Makes a Dakota blind?"

"I am not blind to the evil deeds of the white people," said Jean Baptiste. "I choose to follow the Jesus way, not the white man's way."

"Then you *are* blind!" said Kaduza. "They will not let you be one without the other. If you choose the white man's way, they force their religion upon you. If you choose their religion, they make you live and do as they do."

And so they talked on—sometimes softly, sometimes loudly, sometimes in anger, more often in sadness. When they parted, they were still friends, but the bond that held them now was not so much the bond of fond memories of a happy past as it was a shared despair over a hopeless present.

Jean Baptiste's last words were far from comforting. "The white man's civilization may not be the best, but the Dakota cannot escape it. We must conform to the white man's way peaceably or forcibly. The choice is: conform or be crushed."

"It is very strange," Kaduza said sadly, "but without meaning to you have given me back my purpose, my will to fight. If the white men will not leave our valley peacefully, then they must be forced to leave. They must leave—or be crushed."

The second event that rebuilt Kaduza's will to fight the white men was the last council meeting before the final battle at Wood Lake. It was called by Little Crow in a last desperate attempt to persuade the Wahpetonwan and Sisseton tribes to join the Mdewakantonwan and Wahpekute tribes in their war upon the whites. After the feasting and the smoking came the speeches. Kaduza sat beside Red Beaver, his eyes on the ground, his ears listening intently for words to which his mouth could speak the "*Hau! Hau! Hau!*" of assent.

He did not hear any such words in the speech of the Christian Dakota Paul Mazakutemane, who had been leader of the Hazelwood Republic. It could have been Jean Baptiste speaking. "You Mdewakantonwans and Wahpekutes have been with the white men longer than the Upper Dakota. Yet I who am an Upper

153

Dakota have put on white men's clothes and consider myself a white man. I was very much surprised to learn that you had been killing the settlers, for you had the advice of preachers for so many years. Why did you not tell us you were going to kill them? I ask you the question again: why did you not tell us? The reason was that if you had done so and we had counseled together, you would not have been able to involve our young men with you.

"Men who will cut women's and children's throats are cowards. I am ashamed of you! Give me the captives, and I will take them to Fort Ridgely."

"*Hau! Hau! Hau!*" cried Red Beaver and the Christian Dakota and most of the Upper Reservation Dakotas.

"Kill the captives! Kill the captives!" shouted the younger warriors from the Lower Reservation and many of the young men of the Upper Reservation.

"Mazakutemane says nothing of the white man's shame," muttered Kaduza, but he did not join the chanting.

It was Rdainyanka, son-in-law of the Mdewakantonwan chief Wabasha, who spoke what was in Kaduza's heart. Wabasha had been against the war from the very beginning, but Rdainyanka's speech soon made it clear that he did not share his father-in-law's thoughts. "I am for continuing the war and am opposed to the delivery of the prisoners. I have no confidence that the whites will stand by any agreement they make if we give them up. Ever since we traded with them their agents and traders have robbed and cheated us. Some of our people have been shot, some hanged, others placed upon floating ice and drowned, and many have been starved in their prisons. It was not the intention of the Dakota nation to kill any of the whites until after the four returned from Acton and told what they had done. When they did this, all the young men became excited, and commenced the massacre. The older ones would have prevented it if they could, but since the treaties they have lost all their influence. We may regret what has happened, but the matter has gone too far to be remedied. We have to die. Let us, then,

154

kill as many of the whites as possible, and let the prisoners die with us."

As if they had but one throat, the younger Dakota warriors of all four bands shouted "*Hau! Hau! Hau!*" Kaduza shouted with them, a fierce exultation he had never before known in his heart.

Red Beaver and the older men sat with bowed heads. The vote for continuing the war was carried by the young men. The council meeting broke up, and the young braves rode off singing a Dakota war song.

> Over the earth I come.
> Over the earth I come.
> A soldier I come.
> Over the earth I am a ghost.

"Why doesn't Little Crow attack the Long Trader's men tonight?" fumed Kaduza to Red Beaver as they rode back to Hapanna's lodge. "After all, they sleep but a town-crier's cry away."

"My son forgets that it is deeply lodged in a Dakota's head that if he is killed in the dark he will wander in darkness forever in the Land of Spirits."

Kaduza was asked to serve again as a scout and to watch the Long Trader's movements and warn of a surprise night attack. This time he refused and demanded to be a warrior. His zeal to encounter the enemy in open and fair battle was pitched too high to be content with scouting the enemy. Besides, what was there to scout out? Every move the Long Trader and the Long Knives made was as plain as a herd of buffalo on the prairie.

According to Little Crow's plan, the attack was to be an ambush. While the Long Knives slept, the Dakota warriors quietly took up their three hidden positions—alongside a road the Long Trader's troops would have to use as they moved northward, in a deep ravine near the lake, and behind a hill to the west. Kaduza, stripped down to his breech clout and his body painted like an eclipse of the sun—half black, half red—was assigned to the ravine.

155

It was a good plan, but the Long Knives did not act according to plan. They did not strike camp at dawn as expected but went about laughing and singing as if on an outing. Then four or five wagonloads of soldiers spoiled everything by starting out to the Yellow Medicine Agency to dig potatoes in the Dakota gardens. The warriors concealed in the grass had to rise and fire or be driven over by the wagons. Thus the battle was begun in a place and in a manner Little Crow had not expected.

Being out too far, hundreds of the Dakota warriors did not get into the brief intense battle or fire a shot. Kaduza and the warriors hidden in the ravine were in the thickest of the battle and fought bravely, but the Long Knives' artillery firing from the head of the ravine kept the Dakota from advancing into the camp.

"*Hokahe! Hokahe!* It's a good day to die!" Kaduza shouted as he rose from his hiding place to attack. He kept on shouting that cry as the bullets whizzed past his head like dry leaves in the first blizzard of the winter. The cry died on his lips only when he saw Other Day exuberantly leading the attack. Other Day, clothed in white, a handkerchief knotted around his head, his eyes ablaze, his teeth parted, his face glowing with the joy of battle, was leading the attack—*but on his own Dakota brothers!* He looked the perfect ideal of the Dakota warrior attacking his ancient enemy, but Other Day was attacking his *brothers!*

Kaduza's war cry choked in his throat and his rifle dropped to his side. A thought flashed into his mind like lightning. "So this is what it is to be a Christian! This traitor, this betrayer of his people, is a Christian!"

Suddenly Kaduza's passion to avenge the white men's wrongs to the Dakota and kill as many white men as he could vanished and was replaced by a passion to avenge the Dakota warriors being killed by their own Dakota brother, Other Day. But before his eyes could find that bounding white figure in the chaos and confusion, a bullet struck him in the back of his head and he fell, his head cradling on the shoulder of a fallen Wahpetonwan warrior.

21

So This, Then, Was the Meaning!

Two sleeps later Kaduza awoke on a buffalo robe on the earthen floor of his mother's log lodge. He opened his eyes and saw the faces of his grandmother, mother, sister, and Red Beaver floating and fading and floating again before him. He raised himself on one elbow and fell back again, groaning. "So I cannot even die like a good Dakota warrior!"

Uncida, who was keeping vigil at his bedside and weeping in sorrow, now began weeping for joy. "My grandson lives! My grandson lives again!"

A remembering dream flitted through Kaduza's head and he saw again Other Day's exalted, exuberant face in the battle. "My little grandmother," he whispered, "there is no truth in anyone. There is no sacred way. There is nothing but lies, lies, lies."

"Shuh, shhuh, shuhuh!" sang Uncida, crooning the calming song she had crooned to him as a child. "You are having a bad dream."

"Life is a bad dream," whispered Kaduza. "I want to die. I hoped to die in battle."

Hapanna came swiftly to his side with a bowl of something warm and minty and fragrant. "My son, drink this," she pleaded.

Kaduza obediently drank the bittersweet broth and almost instantly fell into deep sleep, a true sleep. He slept through another sleep and awoke with clear eyes, ears, and head. Hearing

157

a low wailing from Uncida's bed near the door, he raised himself on his elbow. There was no one in the room but Uncida, and Uncida was weeping.

"Uncida, my grandmother," he called in a strong voice, "your grandson is not dead. He will bring buffalo meat to your *tipi* again, and you will bring him moccasins. Everything will be as before—only better."

Uncida's low wailing became a loud wailing. "My grandson, my tears are for the children, the white children you brought us."

"Has Little Crow killed the captives?" asked Kaduza in sharp alarm.

"The Long Trader has made us give up all our white children and women! My daughter your mother and my son-in-law your father have taken the children to the Long Knives' camp. Snana has to give up her daughter who already calls her mother."

Kaduza's first reaction was relief, for he had not actually wanted the captive women and children to be killed. But with the realization of what giving up the captives meant came gloom and despair. So the battle was lost! Then all was lost—forever!

Uncida stopped her wailing and gave her attention to feeding Kaduza, who had not eaten for five days. Kaduza ate silently, and Uncida, who had her own sorrows, respected his silence. When the sun was low in the west, Hapanna and Red Beaver returned from the Long Knives' camp, where 269 captives, both white and half-breed, had been released to the Long Trader. Kaduza broke his silence and asked question after question, and each answer plunged him into deeper gloom.

It seemed that he had been hit in the back of the head by a stray Dakota bullet, a "rotten and spent" bullet, according to Red Beaver, a no-good bullet that did not pierce the skull but put his spirit to sleep and made his body like dead. Chief Mankato had been hit by a spent cannon ball he had seen coming but was too proud to dodge. Sixteen Dakota had been killed and many wounded, but all the wounded had been carried away. Red Beaver had searched for and found Kaduza and carried him off the battlefield.

"Other Day?" asked Kaduza.

"Other Day made great glory for himself with the white men."

"Little Crow?"

Little Crow had collected the Dakotas who were still loyal to him and they and their families had gone west to the Dakota prairies. Many had been taken prisoner. Many had surrendered, for they had been assured that if they did so they would not be punished.

"So this is the end!" said Kaduza.

"My son, if it were only the end!" said Red Beaver.

In the silence of their gloom, Kaduza and Red Beaver heard Uncida scold Hapanna.

"My daughter, you should not have dressed the little white girl in the ugly old clothes she came to us in. She was so pretty in her Dakota dress and leggings!"

"My mother," said Hapanna, 'it would have made your heart both laugh and cry to see how she clung to my neck and would not let the Long Knife take her."

"*Haun-n-n!*" mourned Uncida.

A few days later Samuel J. Brown, son of the former agent and a fluent speaker of the Dakota language, came to the Dakota along the Yellow Medicine and announced that they were all to come to the agency the next morning and be counted by Agent Galbraith for the new annuity roll. At long last they would receive the annuity money! Early the next morning they flocked to the fire-gutted warehouse to be counted. They found Agent Galbraith, the military commander, and clerks sitting at tables outside the stone walls of the warehouse. When Uncida's family—Hapanna, Winona, Jane, Nancy, Gray Whirlwind, Red Beaver, and Kaduza—moved up to the table, a clerk counted them all on his fingers with a flourish. He motioned the women and children to go on, but a soldier stepped up and escorted the three men to the other end of the long building, where Samuel Brown asked them to step inside and be counted as heads of families to receive an extra payment. Before they stepped through the door, Brown took whatever weapons they were carrying and threw them into a barrel, telling them that they would be returned shortly. The three men stepped through the door into the hands of soldiers, who chained them by their ankles, two by two. Kaduza was chained to Red Beaver. Neither betrayed surprise or anger but stood straight and tall and contemptuous.

Kaduza, however, could not restrain his bitterness long. "My father, it seems to make no difference at all to the Long Knives whether we have been friends or foes. You, my father, have always been a man of peace. You have honored the white man's ways your heart told you were better than the Dakota ways. Gray Whirlwind has long been an all-the-way Christian. My mother boasts that he can recite all the names of the little books in the Holy Book. But I—my heart has always said a strong no to both their ways and their religion. I have fought them."

"*Ho-ye!*" exclaimed Red Beaver. "My son even killed a wounded cow!"

"And yet," continued Kaduza, paying no attention to Red Beaver's ironic remark, "yet all three of us are put in chains. For me, perhaps, it is just. For you and Gray Whirlwind it is unjust."

The gloom and anxiety came when they heard the mourning of the women and children after they had discovered what had happened to their fathers and husbands and sons. What would happen to their families now, now that the lies about the annuities were plain to everyone? And what did the whites intend to do with them, the prisoners?

Two hundred thirty-six Dakota males were shackled at the Yellow Medicine Agency that day. The rumors with respect to their fate were almost as numerous. They were all to be executed at dawn the next morning. They were going to be marched to Fort Ridgely and executed there by the soldiers. They were going to be tortured to death slowly by the white settlers who had lost relatives in the uprising. They would be tried by the Long Knives' laws of war, and those who had fought in fair and open battle would be released and those who had murdered and looted in private war parties would be executed. Their families would be sent south to be slaves of the white men.

"Our Father in heaven!" prayed Gray Whirlwind. "Have mercy upon us!"

"My brother, if we have a Father in heaven," said Kaduza not

160

unkindly, "if we have a Father in heaven he must be very partial. He seems to love his white children and hate his red children."

October, the moon when at Lac qui Parle they had dried the rice, the moon when the sugar trees flamed, the moon when the ducks and geese called overhead and rested on Big Stone and Lac qui Parle at night and could be shot for winter food before they rose in flight at dawn—the golden moon of October passed unnoticed by the Dakota. Even Uncida felt no sacredness that autumn, felt only that the Great Spirit had turned his back on his red children. "We are like birds with broken wings!" she wept.

By mid-October the Long Trader had 400 Dakota males in irons at Yellow Medicine and at Camp Release, as his camp where the captives had been released was now called. His military tribunal had begun to sit in judgment on the prisoners and to sentence them to death or imprisonment, but with winter coming he sensed the impossibility of feeding 3600 soldiers, condemned prisoners, and women and children so far from the source of supplies. Court was suspended and everyone was moved down the river to the ruins of the Lower Agency.

"It is only fitting," thought many a Minnesota government official, soldier, and citizen, "for there is where the whole demonic affair started. Let the savage maniacs be tried at the scene of their crime!"

By mid-October Kaduza and Red Beaver were so wordlessly weary of squatting on an earthen floor, ankles chained together, heads bent, blankets drawn over their updrawn knees, that they welcomed the trek down the river. The hardest ordeal was passing the encampment of women and children along the road and hearing the wailing. The cavalry soldiers flanking the prisoners prevented the women and children from approaching their husbands and fathers and sons, but their piercing cries reached their ears. Many prisoners were sure that they heard the voices of their dear ones. Kaduza was sure that he recognized Uncida's voice. "*Mitakoza!* My grandson!"

Kaduza, Red Beaver, and Gray Whirlwind were tried in a

161

group of eight in the kitchen of Trader LaBathe's partly destroyed house at the Lower Agency. By this time the commissioners were weary of hearing protestations of innocence from their prisoners and were interested only in "Were you there? Were you in any one of the major battles?" Gray Whirlwind said that he had taken part in no battle, and no one could testify that he had. Moreover, Missionary Riggs, who was present at all the trials as interpreter and identifier, said that he was a very faithful member of the church at Yellow Medicine. Gray Whirlwind was released to join the innocent prisoners, including Hapanna, Uncida, Winona, and his children. A Christian Dakota testified that he had seen Red Beaver on the battlefield at Wood Lake. When asked if that was true, Red Beaver quietly assented.

"Only to seek the wounded!" protested Kaduza, but since he was only a prisoner, no one in the tribunal paid any attention to him, especially when it was learned that neither Kaduza nor Red Beaver was a member of any Christian church. Red Beaver was sentenced to be hanged.

Kaduza confessed to taking part in all the major engagements of the uprising. One alone was sufficient to convict him. The testimony of She Gathers Huckleberries that she had heard him say that he had killed and scalped was quite unnecessary, as was another's testimony that he was a member of the secret Warrior Lodge on the Lower Reservation. Kaduza was sentenced to be hanged.

Of the 392 Dakota males tried by the tribunal in that month, 303 were sentenced to be hanged. It was the intention of General Pope, commander of the Northwest Department of the Military, of Alexander Ramsey, governor of Minnesota, and of Henry Sibley, now promoted to brigadier general, that the condemned men be executed at once. Their names were telegraphed to President Lincoln. On November 10 President Lincoln telegraphed back asking for the full and complete records of the court-martial proceedings against the condemned men.

Kaduza was not surprised by the sentence to be hanged. In fact, he had expected it from the time he and his Dakota brothers had been hoaxed into their chains. Moreover, he and every other intelligent Dakota now realized the ferocity of the hatred the whites felt for any and all Indians. Sheer and utter detestation looked at them from the face of every white settler brought in to identify the malefactors. By comparison, the bored faces of the soldier guards looked cordial and kind, and some of the prisoners began to look upon them as their protectors from lynching mobs. To Kaduza, however, it made no difference whether he was lynched unlawfully by an angry mob or lynched lawfully by the Long Knives. He did not fear death. It was not his approaching death that threw him into deepest despair. It was the death that had already happened, the death of all meaning, the death of all purpose, the death of all his singing dreams, the death of all hope. Yet it was not so much the death of *his* meanings, *his* purpose, *his* dream, and *his* hope that darkened his spirit and made him unable to speak to Red Beaver, manacled to his heart as well as to his ankle, as it was the death of all meaning for Uncida. It was Uncida who was in his day thoughts and night thoughts now. Uncida, for whom life had been a gift. Uncida, who saw sacred truths in everything, in seeds and seedlings, in dragonflies and morning mists. Uncida, who sang her prayers and prayed her songs. Uncida, who was the living symbol of the Dakota sacred beliefs. Uncida, who he was sure, could not bear the death of all her meanings and dreams and hopes. If *they* died, Uncida would die. If *they* died, what remained of Uncida's life would be ashes.

When Kaduza learned that the very next day 1800 of the "innocent" prisoners were to be escorted by soldiers on the long walk from their camp nearby to a prison camp below Fort Snelling, his despair bordered on insanity. He leaped to his feet in the crowded log jail where they were being kept and shouted at the top of his lungs.

Cursed be the white men!
Cursed be the destroyers!
Cursed be the destroyers of the great Dakota nation!
Cursed be they who send our loved ones far away!
Cursed be they who send us to our death and will not let us say farewell to our loved ones!

163

"*Wahn! Wahn!*" cried some of the prisoners in surprise, for Kaduza was known as a silent one.

But the majority of the prisoners cried the Dakota man's expression of sorrow, "*Hunhunhe!*" until their cries sounded like a great amen to Kaduza's curses.

Kaduza dropped to the earthen floor and buried his head on his drawn-up knees. Red Beaver placed his arm around the young man's shoulders and bent his head to Kaduza's in grief.

Thus they did not see the tall young white man admitted to the prison by a guard. The white man asked something of a prisoner near the door, who pointed toward Kaduza. The young man stepped carefully past the squatting, sprawling prisoners and dropped to his knees before Kaduza and Red Beaver. "Kaduza, my brother, is it you?"

Kaduza slowly raised his head from his knees and looked searchingly into the other's face for any true thing it might have to give—if there be any true thing in this life. "John? You came back? You know what has happened, and still you came back?"

"I came back as soon as I heard in Ohio what had happened here. I had to come back, for many of you Mdewakantonwans and Wahpekutes are my friends. Today I came to find you especially, Kaduza. I came to thank you for coming to warn me before dawn that morning. Napesni told me that you came."

"John," said Kaduza urgently, "my grandmother, my mother, my sister and her family go tomorrow on the long walk to Fort Snelling. My father Red Beaver and I are to die. Will you take messages from us to them?"

"Can you write? I shall bring you paper."

"I have not learned to write or to read," said Kaduza. "But Red Beaver, my father, can. Your own father taught him."

"Good! I remember you now, Red Beaver. I shall bring you paper, and you, Kaduza, can tell Red Beaver what you want him to write. I shall bring the letter to your family myself. Perhaps you do not know it, but I shall be walking all the way with your family. Our Lord Jesus Christ has given me all these innocent prisoners to love and to care for. I will never leave them."

Kaduza looked at John incredulously. His heart could not believe what his ears were hearing, but since his heart hungered to believe what his ears were hearing, his heart believed.

Suddenly Kaduza's vision on the bluffs above the Standing Rock River flashed into his mind. He saw once more the space that fell from the cliff to the river burst into a huge fire, the kind the white men make. The huge leaping fire had died down to a bed of ashes. Two shadow-figures knelt on the opposite sides of the ugly bed of ashes. John Williamson and himself! The shadow-figure of John Williamson had slowly and deliberately raised itself on its hands and walked around the ugly ash heap, waving its legs in the air. John Williamson performing the *heyoka* ceremony around the ashes of a huge wildfire! He saw the Holy Sun Dance Tree grow straight and tall out of the ugly ash heap and saw John Williamson rise erect and become a Sun Dancer.

So this, then, was the meaning of his vision! John Williamson was a *heyoka*, a *heyoka* in real life, acting contrary to all the other whites! John Williamson was at the same time a Sun Dancer, dancing in pain for the good of the innocent Dakota prisoners! So *this* was the meaning!

22

To See That,
They Need the
Crossed Eyes of a *Heyoka*

On the seventh day of November, the Moon When the Deer Rut, 1800 Dakota women, children, half-breeds, old men, and a handful of young men considered wholly innocent started the long walk from the Redwood Agency to Fort Snelling. They were accompanied on their walk by the Reverend John Williamson of the Presbyterian mission and the Reverend Samuel Hinman of the Episcopal mission. Not many soldier-guards escorted them, for, after all, nine out of ten were either women or children. They walked in Dakota fashion, single file, and carried their small children, *tipis*, kettles, and the remnants of their possessions. The scraggly forlorn procession stretched over four miles and wound across the prairie that less than two months before had been savaged and ravaged by painted Dakota warriors. Yet many of those who walked their last journey across the valley of the Minnesota knew that most of the men who had taken active part in that mad attack on isolated settlers had fled west or north and were now beyond the reach of the Long Trader and his soldiers.

At Henderson hundreds of white men, women, and children attacked the four-mile-column with clubs, knives, guns, and stones. The guards, who had thought themselves guarding white civilians from their savage prisoners, suddenly found themselves guarding their Indian prisoners from the savage whites. When the guards finally managed to drive back the attackers and get the procession moving along the trail again, many an old woman and old man nursed stab wounds and battered heads. A baby torn from its mother's arms by an infuriated attacker was so badly maltreated that it soon died and was laid on the crotch of a tree along the trail. The young mother was too stunned to sing a death song, but Uncida's words were heard above the shuffling feet as the procession moved along. "Weep not for her! Our little sister will taste no more the miseries of this life. Weep for ourselves! For we are orphans." The word *orphan* was picked up and repeated from mouth to mouth until the great long line of prisoners was chanting it in unison:

> *Wamdenica!*
> *Wamdenica!*
> *Wamdenica!*

The mounted white guards nervously wondered if this was another one of the savages' war songs. The only two other white men walked with bowed heads.

If Kaduza had heard Uncida's words that day, he would have known immediately that her singing dreams had died and that this was the death song of her dreams. But Kaduza was on his own journey to death, for he and Red Beaver and 303 condemned men, 17 women to do the cooking for them, four children, and four Friendlies, all under guard and shackled in crowded wagons, were on their way to Camp Lincoln, a hastily constructed prison camp at the mouth of the Blue Earth River near Mankato. Kaduza sat hunched against the November cold, deep in his own thoughts, and was hardly aware of what was taking place.

The great conflagration in his vision! That was plain to understand. It was the brief but violent outbreak that had swept the valley of the Minnesota like a prairie fire. As to who had kindled the fire, of that there was no doubt in his mind: the white man's greed, the white man's cheating and lying in his dealings with the Dakota, his contempt for the Dakota. As for the ashes, that was the death and devastation—not least, the death of the Dakota nation.

167

But John Williamson a *heyoka?* Today the meaning was not as clear to him as it had been for a brief moment that day when the young missionary had told him that he would be walking all the way from the Redwood Agency to Fort Snelling with his family. A *heyoka?* A *heyoka* who walked through the steam of a boiling kettle and called it a cold wind, who called boiling water freezing, who sat in snow and fanned himself, who sat in summer heat and shivered? A *heyoka* who at feasts stood on his moccasinned hands and ate? A *heyoka* who rode his horse sitting backward, who strung his arrows against himself? A *heyoka* who danced and clowned to appease the flying mystery in the sky, the lightning the thunder being had used to kill his father? A *heyoka* who took the most humiliating role in life, who laid himself open to ridicule? Was John Williamson truly such a person? Was John Williamson a *heyoka,* a contrary? Or a Sun Dancer? It was no secret that the missionaries thought the Sun Dance was an invention of an Evil One. And John Williamson was a missionary!

So lost in his thoughts was Kaduza that he had not noticed that the procession of prisoners and guards had come to New Ulm, which had been attacked twice by the Dakota, had suffered 32 dead and 60 wounded, and lost one-third of its houses by fire. Hearing the shouts of alarm from both prisoners and guards, Kaduza raised his head and saw the road through town lined with women waiting for the condemned men with buckets of boiling water, pitchforks, hoes, bricks, and stones. Their faces contorted with fury and screaming their hatred, they threw their missiles and wielded their weapons. Kaduza warded off a slashing scissors by seizing the wrist of his assailant and for a brief moment looked into a face so distorted with lust for revenge that it did not look human. A guard pulled the woman back from the wagon and was slashed in the wrist. The wounds were many and painful before the teamsters got the wagons out of New Ulm. Red Beaver nursed a bruised jaw.

"White women are better fighters than their men," he mused.

Kaduza's thoughts darted back to the question in his mind. Was John truly a *heyoka?* The hate-contorted face of the German women had answered his question and confirmed that flash of insight he had had when John had told him that he would never leave the innocent prisoners. The scissor-wielding New Ulm woman had acted according to the ancient and universal laws of vengeance. Her husband had no doubt been killed by a Dakota. It was perfectly normal for her to want to kill an Indian, any or all Indians. For John Williamson, however, it was altogether abnormal, it was *contrary* to the normal for him to be walking this very day and hour with the 1800 hated and despised Indians whose only crime was that they were relatives of the condemned Dakota. What was it John had said? "Our Lord Jesus Christ has given me these innocent prisoners to love and to care for, and I shall never leave them." *Ho!* John was truly a *heyoka,* and Kaduza's vision had told the truth! But only half the truth, for in his dream vision he had seen himself rise up on moccasinned feet and follow John around the ugly bed of ashes. And he, Kaduza, was certainly no *heyoka.* Nor would he ever dance the Sun Dance. If his legs did any dancing, they would dance at the end of the hangman's noose! As for John dancing the Sun Dance, no missionary would ever dance a dance considered so unholy.

Camp Lincoln was the name of the crude, drafty, and barely finished stockade in which Kaduza and his fellow prisoners were placed. Here they sat and ate and slept in a sprinkling of straw on the earthen floor and suffered the combined effects of severe cold, inactivity, and a diet of hard bread and beef. No effort was made to secure the barn-like structure against the cold November winds or to improve their diet, for in the minds of both captors and captives the condemned men would be executed any day now. Any day now a telegram from President Lincoln would cure their coughs and colds and constipation forever. The two men who died from their injuries at the hands of the enraged New Ulm women did not make any real difference. Two less to hang!

Visitors began at once to walk the narrow aisle down the middle of the two sections of the building and to gawk at the condemned men. As they passed, prisoners sometimes leaned toward them and softly spoke in Dakota what seemed to be words of friendly greeting but actually were bitter words. "Whom have you come to see?" asked Rdainyanka, Chief Wabasha's son-in-law, who had spoken eloquently for continuing the war. "Have you come to see rapists? Go look at your own Long Knives, who think our wives and daughters exist only for their pleasure. Have you come to see murderers and killers? Go look at the Long Knives of the North and of the South and see how they are killing each other by the thousands."

"*Hau! Hau! Hau!*" murmured the prisoners close enough to hear him.

The visitors walked on without having understood a word.

One of the first to come and one of the only ones who did not gawk was Dr. Thomas Williamson. As soon as he heard of the arrival of the prisoners, he hurried from St. Peter, where he had decided to live, to Mankato. Because he was a personal friend of General Sibley, he was granted permission to enter the stockade and to speak with the prisoners. He moved slowly down the aisle, stopping to greet Dakota he knew by name and at intervals to raise his voice and tell his listeners that their chains were not the worst chains that held them. Everyone, he said, red or white, was bound in the chains of sin. The one Great God had sent his Son to free men from the chains of sin. His Son Jesus Christ had the power to free them forever from the chains of sin.

"If the Great God could take away the chains on my legs, I would listen with my heart as well as with my ears," muttered a prisoner on Kaduza's right.

Kaduza, who two weeks ago would have said the same thing or something more biting, raised his hand to silence him so that he could hear Missionary Williamson's words more clearly. When Dr. Williamson finally stood before him and Red Beaver, Kaduza searched his face urgently. Was the father, too, a *heyoka*, a contrary? Did he, too, think and act just the opposite of everyone else? The eyes that looked down at him were warm with recognition and sad with realization. The father of John was indeed a *heyoka!*

"I am truly sad to see Sarah's son and Sarah's husband here!"

"Dr. Williamson, can you take a letter to them? John carried a letter to them from us at Redwood," said Red Beaver.

"I shall bring paper the next time I visit you."

"If there is a next time for us!" muttered the prisoner on Kaduza's right.

There was a next time—in fact, many next times, for the telegram from President Lincoln authorizing the mass execution did not come. But Kaduza did not even wait for Missionary Williamson's prompt return visit. Ignoring the teasing of his fellow prisoners, he asked Red Beaver to begin to teach him how to read and to write at once. He swept the straw away from the earthen floor between his legs and asked his teacher to trace the letters in the dirt, erasing them when his quick mind had memorized their shapes. In less than an hour he could read and write the words for mother, father, sister, and grandmother.

"Why learn to read and write when tomorrow you die?" asked his neighbor.

"Does not every Dakota believe that in the Land of Spirits we will do what we were doing when we died? Is that not the reason we have wanted to die in battle rather than to die in bed?" Kaduza responded.

"Does my son no longer believe it is most glorious to die on the battlefield?" asked Red Beaver.

"There is another way," answered Kaduza simply.

Missionary Williamson returned with paper and pencils for those who could write and wished to write letters. He had slates for those who wished to learn. To the amazement of the prisoners, his sister Jane came with him and walked down the aisle helping him to distribute the paper.

She smiled down at Kaduza and Red Beaver. "I remember you from Kaposia! Julia's brother and Sarah's husband. Would you like paper to write to them? My brother will bring the letters to John, and John will give them to your family. John is with them, you know."

"We know!" they said.

"Another *heyoka*," thought Kaduza. "A woman *heyoka!*"

Missionary Williamson stopped to talk to them and, at Red

171

Beaver's request on Kaduza's behalf, left a frayed copy of the book of Mark in the Dakota language. It was the first book he and Missionary Riggs and Joseph Renville had translated together.

"Your *koda*-friend Jean Baptiste Renville has asked me to bring you special greetings. He and his wife have been with us these days. His heart is sad that you are here. He feels that you are wrongfully here. He feels that you have refused to speak in your own defense."

Every Saturday Missionary Williamson walked to Mankato and preached to the prisoners. When he went back to St. Peter, he carried letters from the prisoners to their families at Fort Snelling. By the first week of the Moon When the Deer Shed Their Horns he carried Kaduza's first letter written in his own hand.

My grandmother,
My mother,
My sister,
you are very dear to me but you will see me no more.
My heart tells me that Wakantanka
and the Great God are the same God.
I trust in him.
Do not sorrow for me.

Kaduza

On December 4 frustrated citizens impatient for the extermination of the savages marched to the stockade to take things into their own hands. However, they were held back and turned away by the guards. Governor Ramsey, General Sibley, and General Pope renewed their pressure on the president to order the execution of the criminals at once or risk the danger of having both camps of prisoners wiped out by angry mobs.

General Sibley moved the prisoners from Camp Lincoln into a more secure log prison in a vacant lot between two buildings in the town of Mankato. It was built of large logs. The walls were only four feet high, and there was no room for the prisoners to move about, only enough for them to sit and to lie down.

On December 6 President Lincoln in his own handwriting wrote an order to General Sibley to execute only 39 of the 303 condemned prisoners and cited them by name and by number. He and his lawyers had not found enough evidence in the military records to justify executing the 264 other men on grounds of rape and murder. The Minnesota citizens were furiously disappointed and blamed the bleeding hearts out East for softening the president's heart—but prepared for the gratifying spectacle of seeing at least 39 savages hanged.

The Reverend Stephen Riggs, missionary to the Dakota people since 1837, was asked to assist Joseph R. Brown, a former agent, to identify the 39 to be hanged. They were removed from the jail to tighter security, and the president's order was read to them. They listened in silence and then broke into a Dakota death song. Fearing the chant was a war song, the guards chained the 39 to the floor and called for extra guards.

One of the 39 was reprieved at the last minute by President Lincoln. It was Round Wind, whom Kaduza had known at Lac qui Parle. Now an old man, he had been wrongfully accused by two immigrant German boys of killing their mother. But Round Wind was known by the missionaries to have been on the other side of the Minnesota River at the time the boys said their mother was killed. It was a letter from Aunt Jane to President Lincoln that brought the last-minute reprieve.

Missionaries Riggs and Williamson and two Catholic priests prepared the 38 for death. Thirty-six asked for and received Baptism. One of the two who did not said that he had two wives, both of them good women, and several children who had gone to the Spirit Land, and he wished to be with them and not be separated from them in the white man's heaven.

As the 38 prisoners marched to the scaffold on that bitterly cold December day, the day after Christmas, they chanted a song.

Kaduza and Red Beaver, still shackled together, leaned against the wall of the prison and peered through the cracks at the entire ritual. The loud wailing of the Dakota women who cooked for the prisoners and of their children rose above the chant.

173

"What are our Dakota brothers singing?" asked Kaduza, who did not recognize this particular death song of his people.

"Hapanna has sung it many times," said Red Beaver quietly. "It is a hymn from the Dakota Hymn Book prepared by the missionaries and Joseph Renville at Lac qui Parle. Our brothers are singing to the Great God and asking him to bless them with life that has no end, eternal life with him."

As the 38 mounted the scaffold and the soldiers began placing the death hoods over their heads, the wailing of the Dakota women and children became piercing shrieks.

"Hear me, my people!" cried a voice from the scaffold, and his words soared above the cries of grief.

"Who is it?" asked Kaduza.

"I cannot tell."

"Hear me, my people!" cried the voice. "Listen to my words carefully. Do not mourn for us. Let your tears be tears of joy, for this is not a day of defeat but a day of victory! We have made our peace with God and now go to be with him forever. Tell our children and their children to remember this day. We are honorable men who fought for a just cause. We are not criminals."

The 38 death hoods were placed over the 38 heads. A drum was sounded. The father of two victims of the uprising cut the rope that dropped the platform and the 38 Dakota to their deaths.

Kaduza and Red Beaver turned abruptly away from the crack between the logs of their prison.

"He was as innocent as you and I," said Kaduza bitterly, after a long silence.

"Which one? There were several out there on that scaffold who were as innocent as you and I," said Red Beaver.

"Rdainyanka. He could have ecaped to Canada or the western prairies along with Little Crow, Sacred Battle, Pawn, and Mazzawaninuna. He could be safe now if Wabasha, his father-in-law, had not told him to give himself up to the whites for no innocent Dakota would be harmed."

"He could be safe with the four young Dakota who started it all by arguing about eggs," said Red Beaver.

174

"Do you think, my son," asked Red Beaver after another long silence, "that those white people looking on and filling their eyes with the sight of Dakota braves dying have the eyes to see that those Dakota braves have human feelings? That they hold life dear? That they love their wives and children? That they faced death fearlessly like true Dakota braves but were full of fears and sorrow for their families? Do you suppose that these white people looking on have eyes to see that?"

"A white person who would see that would have to have crossed eyes," said Kaduza. "He would have to have the eyes of a *heyoka*."

23

This Is Indeed
a New Thing

The remaining prisoners in the log jail at Mankato had not expected one more winter to be added to their winter count. If they had expected another winter, they most certainly would have expected a desolate, sad, and bitter one, a nothing-to-do, the-world-has-ended-for-us winter. Physically, the winter of 1862-63 was all of that and more for them. The earthen floor was cold, the straw thin, the fires were small and far between, and their issue of one blanket per prisoner insufficient for a Minnesota winter.

Mentally and spiritually, the winter of 1862-63 was unlike any winter these Dakota men had ever experienced. For almost every man chained in that Mankato prison it seemed as if a bonfire had been kindled in his mind and spirit. The bonfire burned with such intensity that most were unaware of guards being changed and of curious visitors walking up and down the aisle between the rows of prisoners. Everyone but the very old with rheumy eyes became an ardent pupil of the few prisoners who could read and write the Dakota language.

Chaske, who had been taught by Missionaries Williamson and Riggs and baptized Robert Hopkins, after the missionary drowned at Traverse des Sioux, became the leader in the prison. Why he was a prisoner at all remained something of a mystery, for he had been a faithful member of the church at Yellow Medicine and had personally saved Dr. Williamson, his wife,

176

and Aunt Jane from certain death. But after rescuing them, his insatiable curiosity about what was happening had taken him to the attack on Fort Ridgely and New Ulm. There was enough evidence, true or false, to keep him in prison after his reprieve from execution by President Lincoln. It was Robert Hopkins Chaske who, between Missionary Williamson's visits, woke his fellow prisoners early in the morning to the singing of hymns from the Dakota Hymn Book and to prayers. At first only the few church members offered prayers, but more and more prisoners joined in the public praying—praying not only for themselves and absent families but also for the soldier guards, the officers, the Great Father in Washington, and all the white people who were angry with them and wished to destroy them. At sundown Robert Hopkins Chaske led them again in evening worship. In between, the prisoners scarcely raised their eyes from their books and slates. By midwinter, Dakota who on the first day of January could not say the letters of the Dakota alphabet were sending letters to their relatives at Fort Snelling, some of them written in a beautiful hand. Many of the letters pleaded that those who received the letters might also listen to the missionaries' teachings and learn to read and to write.

Kaduza was himself too intensely interested in learning to read and write to be amazed at either his fellow prisoners or at himself, or to wonder why this sudden hunger to hear and to read the teaching from the white man's Holy Book. He wasted no time in trying to determine whether it was because the white man's spirit power had proved to be stronger than their own spirit powers and because the *wakan* power of their medicine men and war prophets had failed them. Or whether it was simply because the sight of 38 of their brothers dangling from beams, their faces hidden in white death caps, had struck terror into their hearts and they were desperately falling over themselves in their haste to leave the Red Man's Road and travel the White Man's Road. Or whether it was because the red man's tomorrow had been snatched from their hearts and they were grasping at the white man's tomorrow. Or whether it was fear of the white man's hell. Or whether it was just a desire to learn means of communicating with the loved ones at Fort Snelling.

Such thoughts were like noisy blackbirds flying helterskelter in his mind. If there were to be birds in his mind, he wanted them to be silent and to fly in the shape of the letters of the Dakota alphabet.

Learning to read was amazingly easy for Kaduza. Once he had learned the sounds of the letters, the words rose on swift wings from the page. Against Red Beaver's advice he began at once to read the frayed copy of the book of Mark that Missionary Williamson had brought to him. "It is the same as placing a leg of buffalo meat before a blind, helpless, newborn puppy and telling it to eat," said Red Beaver.

"But this puppy is not blind," said Kaduza.

To Kaduza's delight the words he pronounced—at first stumblingly, phonetically, laboriously, were not the words of a strange language but the words of the language of his childhood, the language of his heart. In the very first chapter he read:

"Unkan mahpiya eciyatanhan wicaho wan tanin, Micinksi wastewakidake can tanyan iyomakipi kin he niye ce." ("And a voice came from heaven, 'Thou art my beloved Son; with thee I am well pleased.' ")

Kaduza's heart leaped to hear his mouth pronounce the Dakota word *Micinksi,* my son. He pronounced it again, slowly, relishing each syllable.

How lovingly his own father Strong Heart had said that word to him! And Joseph Renville to Jean Baptiste, when he did not call him his *Koda Mitawa.* But, of course. These words of the heart had to be Dakota words from the heart. Joseph Renville had given the Dakota words to the missionaries. Missionary Williamson had read the words from the French Bible, Joseph Renville had pondered the meaning and then said it in Dakota, and Gideon Pond had written it down. How many snows and winters ago that had been—when he was a man-child and had been called Burning Arrow. And now he was Kaduza and sat in chains in a white man's prison, from which, if the white citizens

178

in the town of Mankato had their will, he and his fellow prisoners would never come out alive.

Kaduza turned away from throwing his thoughts back to his childhood on the Lac qui Parle and stumbled eagerly on with his reading, eager to find the meaning of his vision. He had caught a glimpse of the meaning in John Williamson's face when he had started the long walk with the forlorn families of the condemned Dakota men. And again in the face of the German woman who attacked him on the streets of New Ulm. Glimmers of meaning, but what was the *full* meaning of his vision?

Kaduza plodded on in the book of Mark. It took him several days to come to Chapter 12, where he found with great excitement what he thought was the clue and the connection between his vision and the Holy Book. He read it aloud to Red Beaver: "And one of the scribes came up and heard them disputing with one another, and seeing that he answered them well, asked him, 'Which commandment is the first of all?' Jesus answered, 'Hear, O Israel: The Lord our God, the Lord is one; and you shall love the Lord your God with all your heart, and with all your soul and with all your mind, and with all your strength.' The second is this, 'You shall love your neighbor as yourself.' There is no other commandment greater than these."

"This is the secret of John!" said Kaduza to Red Beaver. "Jesus Christ is like a *heyoka*, and so is John. Jesus loved when others hated. He was tender when others were hard. He was hard when others were soft. He was silent when others chattered. He spoke of the evil in men's hearts when they would rather not hear about it. He spoke of death when they would rather forget it. This is the new vision in the Holy Book. This is the new way of being. It is to be a *heyoka* in the world. It is to be a contrary to the world, to do the opposite of what the world expects!"

"My son, there is nothing new in those commandments," said Red Beaver. "If we seek to the heart of our ancient Dakota religion we find the same two loves commanded. First love to the Great Spirit who has made all things. Then love for all that the highest Spirit has made, all things. *All*, my son! The four-leggeds as well as the two-leggeds. The winged creatures, the trees, grasses. All are our brothers and sisters. This I do not hear in the white man's religion. Nor do I see it in his life. It is true that these commandments are written in the white man's Holy Book, but are they written in the white man's heart?"

"All that you say makes Jesus look more and more like a *heyoka* and his way to be contrary to all other ways," said Kaduza triumphantly.

"I do not deny that," said Red Beaver, "I only deny that this is a new vision of life never before revealed to the heart of man in any way."

So Kaduza plowed on in his tattered copy of the book of Mark. His reading was far easier and faster now. When he finally reached the story of the crucifixion of Christ, the new thing that never arose in the heart of any man, he was so overwhelmed that he sat silent and did not speak of it to Red Beaver until the thoughts that arrived in a jumbled ferment of haste had settled down to some order.

The first thought that exploded in his mind like a spark in parched prairie grass was the thought of Jesus Christ dancing the Sun Dance. Jesus Christ suffering and dancing for the good of each and every one. Sharpened green sticks piercing the tendons of his breast and fastened to a leather thong leading to the Sacred Tree, the Sun Dance Tree, the tall slender cottonwood painted the sacred red color of blood, earth, and sky, the holy Sun Dance Tree with the branches of chokecherries tied across it, forming a cross. Jesus Christ, shuffling around the Sun Dance Tree to the drumbeat of his own heart. Jesus Christ, fainting with weariness, his throat parched with thirst, his breast dripping with great drops of blood from the weight of the buffalo skulls fastened to the thongs and tearing at his flesh.

Son of God is a suffering god! A God who chose of his own free will to live as a human being on this tear-drenched earth, a God who shared man's pain, shared man's sorrow, demanded nothing for himself. A God who died a shameful death on a cross, as shameful a death as being hung from the neck on a scaffold. A God who cried out in the hour of his death: "My God, my God, why hast thou forsaken me?"

180

So the Holy Book of the white man is a book about Wakan-tanka's suffering love for all men! And the crucifixion is a Sun Dance, the greatest Sun Dance in the world, the greatest event in the world, the greatest event of any time or place! Jesus Christ, Son of God, the Sun Dancer for the whole world!

Strange mystery! Strange saving mystery! Strange new power for the powerless ones who cannot help themselves. Strange new way of living, of being. *To suffer with!* To love as one who *suffers with those who suffer!*

In a barely audible voice Kaduza was finally able to tell Red Beaver the thoughts that had unwrapped a great and hidden truth for him. Red Beaver listened quietly and said, quite simply, "My son, that is indeed a new thing."

24

The Sign of Contradiction

In the long winter in the Mankato prison, Sunday became in very fact the sun-day for the prisoners, became the one luminous day in the week that otherwise had no variation. Every Saturday Missionary-Doctor Williamson walked the 13 miles from his new home near St. Peter to the prison at Mankato. In his backpack he carried a bundle of letters from the camp at Fort Snelling, paper and pencils with which the prisoners could answer the letters, copies of books of the Bible in the Dakota language, school books. On the Holy Day, assisted by Robert Hopkins Chaske, he conducted a worship service. Until he returned to St. Peter on Monday or Tuesday, he visited with the prisoners, exhibiting as much interest and concern in their physical as well as their spiritual beings.

From the letters and from talking with Missionary Williamson the prisoners learned that there was the same enthusiasm for hearing the teaching from the Holy Book and for learning to read and to write at the camp down at the mouth of the river as here at the Big Bend. No *tipi* could hold the people crowding to John Williamson's meetings any more. He had received permission to live in the attic room of a large one-story warehouse near the camp and to use it for a meeting house. It was large enough to hold 500 people. Here, crowded under the roof, the relatives of the Mankato prisoners packed the unheated, unlighted room and listened to young John preach and teach. In their *tipis* they practiced making the letters of the Dakota alphabet, learned to make words with them, and soon were able to write to their husbands and sons and brothers at Mankato.

"Your sister Julia is one of the best teachers," said Missionary Williamson.

"My sister was always wanting to teach her younger brother," said Kaduza, "but my heart was not open then to my sister's teaching."

"Is your heart open to Christ your Savior now?" asked Dr. Williamson.

"My heart is open to him now," said Kaduza, not troubling to explain that his heart was open to Jesus Christ as the Sun Dance Savior. He sensed that the gentle missionary would not understand him. Neither would his sister Winona. Would John, his vision-brother?

Now that their ears and hearts were open to the Christian teaching, many of the prisoners who had known and been secretly fond of Gideon Pond over 40 years ago but had resisted his teaching now requested that he come from his parish in Bloomington to visit them.

"Please bring Gideon Pond the next time you come," they told the doctor.

Pond came the next week, his bristling beard now sprinkled with gray. The two shabby, shaggy, loving, and lovable missionaries remained the whole week, and on the following Holy Day in February, the Raccoon Moon, they baptized 274 of the now more than 350 prisoners. Kaduza and Red Beaver knelt together before them. "My brother, this is God's sign which is placed upon you. You will carry it as long as you live. From this time you are to call God your Father. Remember to love him. Be resolved to do his will."

In March, the Moon of Snow Blindness, Missionary Stephen Riggs came along with Dr. Williamson and spent ten days with the prisoners. By the end of that period all the prisoners had asked for and received Baptism. On the following Holy Day the prisoners received the sacrament of Holy Communion. Perhaps some of the simplest minds expected the sacred rite to dissolve

183

their chains. At least one of them, an old man kneeling next to Kaduza, reached for the bread and homemade currant wine and prayed aloud that his chains fall off. Yet the majority of those who received the sacrament that day had a more sophisticated understanding of its meaning. Many of them knew David's psalm of penitence by heart and could sing the Dakota hymn based upon that psalm with genuine fervor:

> *Wakantanka, nitocantekiye on onsimada ye;*
> *Nitowaonsida ota on wawahtani micicajuju wo.*
> (Have mercy on me, O God, according to thy steadfast
>   love;
> according to thy abundant mercy, blot out my
>   transgressions.)

One Holy Day in the Moon of Grass-greening, when buffalo calves are born and the geese lay their eggs, Dr. Williamson preached a sermon on a text that made Kaduza's spirits soar like a redtailed hawk on loftier streams of air. April was a cruel month for the prisoners, for nature was being released from the chains of winter and they were not being released from theirs. Their Dakota blood cried for the sight of open sky, the sound of water running in streamlets, the fragrance of the first prairie flowers, the taste of maple sugar. What the gentle tough missionary said about the text, 1 Corinthians 1:20-26, Kaduza did not remember, but one verse became a litany for his own vision of Christianity: "For the foolishness of God is wiser than men, and the weakness of God is stronger than men."

Foolishness! Weakness! The way of the true follower of Jesus Christ is foolishness, weakness. The way of the *heyoka*. What a strange upside-down teaching!

It became a kind of pastime for Kaduza and Red Beaver to pick out *heyoka* faces among the faces of the visitors who came to the prison—the military and government officials, the reporters, the clergy, the curious. Most of the faces displayed their owner's hatred, some guarded their hatred, some masked their hatred. One notable exception was a face that soon became familiar to the prisoners—the face of the Episcopal Bishop Whip-

184

ple, who came among them with the very same transparent love they saw in the faces of Thomas and John Williamson.

"He is a *heyoka* just like John," said Kaduza.

In the middle of that month, on a day like every other day, Missionary Williamson brought a bundle of letters in which there was a brief note to Kaduza and Red Beaver from Winona telling them that Uncida was dead. It did not surprise them, for rumors had already come to the prisoners of the more than 100 deaths in the camp at Fort Snelling. The very old and the very young had not survived the shuddering cold of the winter and the contagious diseases that swept through the camp.

Since it was impossible to be alone with his grief, Kaduza leaned against the log wall of the prison, closed his eyes and his ears to the world of prison, and threw his thoughts back to the Lac qui Parle and the cottonwood under which he and Uncida had so often talked while she rested from hoeing the corn. Gradually the sounds of the prison faded away and he heard the water kissing the shore of the river Uncida had known and loved so well. As she herself had done so long ago, the memories of Uncida made the silence sing—sing with sadness, sing with joy. Kaduza spoke in his heart to the singing silence.

> Uncida, my little grandmother,
> is your body buried in the ground,
> or did they do as you always wanted
> and as you always believed?
> Did they lay your body on a scaffold
> so that your spirit could easily break its earth bonds?
> Uncida, my little grandmother,
> did they respect the ceremonies you loved?
> Did they honor your Dakota faith?
> Uncida, my little grandmother,
> did they who receive their images from the Sacred Book
> honor the images you received from creation?
> Did they who have their religion written in the Book
> honor the religion you had written in your heart?
> Did they sing the Dakota death songs to you,

185

or did they sing Christian hymns?
Uncida, my little grandmother,
do they think that you are eternally lost—
you who threw away all harsh thoughts,
you who were filled with spirit,
the loving spirit,
the spirit of love?
Uncida, my little grandmother,
if they did not honor your Dakota faith,
he will! He, the Sun Dance Savior.
He danced for you, little grandmother!
And in your honor, little grandmother,
he will fasten a branch of red chokecherries
to the sacred tree, the Holy Tree
his cross!

On the evening of April 21, 1863, by the white man's count, the steamer *Favorite,* returning from delivering supplies to the new military post at the old Redwood Agency, docked at Mankato. Early the next morning four companies of soldiers formed two walls of bayonets from the guardhouse door to the steamer. First to come out were the 15 to 20 women who were to serve as cooks for the prisoners at the destination still unknown to them. Next came the 48 Dakota men who had not been convicted of any crime but had been kept prisoner at Mankato for no good reason whatsoever. They were taken to the boiler deck to be released to the camp at Fort Snelling and to the unknown fate of the families there. Next came the 278 convicted prisoners, once again chained in pairs. These were taken to the lower deck, lit with the red glow of the wood-burning furnaces. They were being spirited away as hastily and secretly as possible to a federal prison at Davenport, Iowa. The haste and secrecy were made necessary by the vindictiveness of the Mankato citizens, who were resolved that the Sioux savages would not leave their town alive.

As soon as the steamer swung into the swift spring current and began the journey downriver, Robert Hopkins Chaske led the prisoners on the lower deck in a service of prayers and hymns. From the Book of Joshua he read: "As I was with Moses, so I will be with you; I will not fail you or forsake you."

The prisoners on the boiler deck joined the prisoners on the lower deck in Missionary Williamson's own hymn:

"Jehowa mayooha, nimayakiye
nitowashte wadowan."
(Jehovah, my Lord, Thou hast saved me,
I sing of thy goodness.)

White people along the banks of the Minnesota heard the singing, saw the red-blanketed Indians, and clustered in excited groups.

"Listen to the dirty red devils sing their war songs!"

"Where are they being taken?"

"The jokers in Washington are probably sending them out to Dakota territory to join the savages that got away! There will be no end to the murdering!"

As the boat neared the sites of their old villages—Shakopee's village, Good Road's village, Black Dog's village—the Dakota grew silent. Dakota from the camp at Fort Snelling who had been permitted to fish from the shore spotted their red-blanketed brothers on the decks of the steamer and with shouts and signals telegraphed the news ahead to the camp. By the time the boat stopped to discharge the 48 prisoners on the boiler deck, every man, woman, and child from the camp was at the dock hoping against hope to see or hear or touch husbands, sons, and brothers. For a few ecstatic moments they believed that all the men were being returned to them. When the 48 had been landed and they saw the plank raised, saw the boat churning off past Pike's Island into the Mississippi, they raised their voices in the most anguished wailing and screaming Kaduza and Red Beaver had ever heard. They did not have to look to know that the anguished women on shore were tearing out their hair in chunks and for want of knives were gashing their flesh with their fingernails.

"Did you see them?" asked Red Beaver in a low voice.

"No," answered Kaduza sadly, "but I saw John."

187

In the throng of Dakota families indistinguishable as a flock of wild geese, he had seen one distinguishable, tall, black-frocked figure—and John's words that day at the Redwood Agency flashed immediately to his mind and comforted him in this darkest moment. "Our Lord Jesus Christ has given me these innocent prisoners to love and to care for, *and I will never leave them.*"

By the time the *Favorite* with its cargo of Dakota prisoners had made the south-bending curve of the Mississippi, St. Paul citizens had been alerted to what was happening and were lining the shores of the river. Hatred the months had moderated flared and flamed again with the knowledge that the Sioux savages were leaving Minnesota without being brought to the gallows. The sounds that struck the ears of the prisoners now were not piercing shrieks of anguish and grief but strident shouts of hatred and frustrated revenge. Stones hurled from the shore fell short and splashed in the water.

Kaduza stood with his arms folded in his blanket and scanned the faces on shore. To his amazement he felt no responding hatred for them. To his amazement and wonder all his hatred of the white men had vanished. Suddenly he saw it for what it was, saw it in the faces of the white people running along the shore, cursing and throwing stones. Pure hatred. Isolated hatred. Hatred that gave birth to hatred. Hatred for hatred. The endless chain of hatred and vengeance. A scalp for a scalp. A life for a life. Dakota against Ojibway, Ojibway against Dakota. Indians against whites, whites against Indians. Whites against whites.

"My heart does not blame them," Kaduza thought to himself. "They are only being true to the way of the world."

Someone—was it Chaske?—began singing Missionary Williamson's hymn. The voices of the prisoners sounded above the raucous shouts from the shore.

"Jehovah, my Lord . . . I sing of thy goodness!"

There is another way, mused Kaduza, who knew the song so well by now that he could think as he sang at the top of his voice. There is a new way of being human, the *heyoka* way, the way of the contrary who goes contrary to the way of the world. And the cross is its sign. The cross is the symbol of the *heyoka* way. The Sacred Tree is the sign of contradiction for the true followers of the Sun Dance Savior. It is the symbol for John's life and the hard road of suffering he is taking with my people. It will be the symbol for my life, too.

But, he thought to himself, as the boat passed the site of Kaposia, Little Crow's village that was no longer there, I shall never forget the drum, the pipe, the old songs. I shall never leave the Good Red Road. For me a branch of chokecherries will always be tied to the cross of Jesus Christ, my Sun Dance Savior.

For one exalted moment Kaduza felt like flipping onto his hands and walking up and down the deck waving his legs and talking the inverse gibberish of the *heyoka*. For one exalted moment he forgot his chains.

Epilog

The ship of prisoners went down the Mississippi and discharged its Dakota passengers at the steamboat landing at Davenport, Iowa. From there they were taken to Camp McClellan, about a mile and a half away, where they were confined in four buildings hastily built of green lumber. Here they were held captive for three years, during which time about 100 of them died and other prisoners were indiscriminately added from time to time as the military saw fit.

As early as May 9, 1863, Dr. Thomas Williamson visited the prisoners, held services, distributed hymnbooks, and ordained ruling elders in the separate bands represented there. The task of the elders was to care for the spiritual life of the prisoners and to conduct classes in reading and writing the Dakota language. Robert Hopkins Chaske quickly came to be regarded by both his brother Dakotas and the white guards as the "preacher and minister" at Camp McClellan during the times when Dr. Williamson was not there. In the next three years Williamson managed to be with the prisoners at least five months out of each year.

In the autumn of 1863, when Dr. Williamson for a short time was forbidden to visit the prisoners by a commander who thought him too friendly to the "savages," Missionary Stephen Riggs, using his influence with General Sibley, was admitted into the prison. In a letter to the American Mission Board he

190

wrote that he firmly believed that if the 250 prisoners were to be tried by a military commission at that time, not one-fifth of them would be convicted. In the same letter he reported that 200 of the prisoners were readers. He also reported that 280 letters had been collected from the prisoners and mailed to their families and friends.

As for those families and friends, approximately 1300 in number, most of them women and children—they passed Davenport in two boats in mid-May of 1863 on their way to an unknown destination "somewhere on the Missouri River." Accompanying the Dakota in the boat *Davenport* were the Episcopal missionary Samuel Hinman and a military escort of 40 men. Accompanying the Dakota in the boat *Northerner* was John Williamson, who had no more idea where the journey would end than did his bewildered and fearful Dakota brothers and sisters. The *Northerner* stopped at the Davenport landing, but the Dakota passengers were not allowed to get off to visit the prisoners. John was permitted to visit them briefly and found them depressed at the thought of their families being sent so far away.

At St. Joseph, Missouri, all 1300 Dakota were loaded on one boat, *Florence,* creating conditions John Williamson bluntly labeled reminiscent of the slave ships. Living on musty hardtack and briny pork with no opportunity to cook, and sleeping in shifts with no room for all to lie down, the families of the prisoners at Davenport arrived at the mouth of Crow Creek in Dakota Territory on June 1.

Gastric illnesses, a miserable starvation diet, and the shock of finding their new home to be a wilderness of dry and dessicated prairie stretching for hundreds of miles brought many of the Dakota, especially the very old and the very young, to their graves. In the three years at Crow Creek 300 of the original 1300 died. Sitting Bull, a Tetonwan Dakota, visited the Crow Creek encampment in the winter of 1863-64 and is said to have resolved then and there to fight the whites to the death, his or theirs.

Since conditions could not possibly improve, they only grew worse. Having arrived too late to plant (nothing would grow

191

anyway) and forbidden weapons of any sort, the Dakota families at Crow Creek would all have died that winter if John Williamson had not persuaded Colonel Thompson, who had selected this site and was in charge of the exiles, to allow 800 of them to go on a buffalo hunt. In the middle of January, thinly-clad, with threadbare tents, two ponies, and a half-dozen guns, the band started off in a northerly direction. They set up their winter camp near the present site of Redfield, South Dakota.

A week later they were eating their fill of buffalo, and the women were happily scraping and tanning hides for moccasins, leggings, and tents. After several weeks the Crow Creek exiles no longer looked sad and emaciated. The voices that joined in the prayers and hymns John Williamson led every morning and evening were strong and confident. When they returned to Crow Creek after a six weeks' absence, they brought meat for those who had been too feeble to go on the hunt. In his *A History of Minnesota* even the historian William Watts Folwell forsakes his scholarly objectivity momentarily and calls John Williamson the Dakota's "Saint John." John's tentmate on this winter hunt was his old friend from Lac qui Parle and the Lower Reservation—Napesni.

In spite of conditions so tragic that the Dakota still speak the name Crow Creek with the same sense of horror that Jews speak of Buchenwald, the interest in Christianity and education at Crow Creek was as high as it was in the camp at Fort Snelling. An average of 100 pupils attended the Crow Creek school. Lacking books, John mixed lampblack with oil and brush-painted words on old newspapers. As soon as a pupil became somewhat proficient, John set him or her to teaching others. The language of instruction was Dakota, for John Williamson and the other Presbyterian missionaries firmly believed that a person's native language is the language that reaches the heart, and that the mind is best reached through the heart. In this practice and in their use of native teachers, both male and female, and in their ordination of native preachers, the

192

Presbyterian missionaries to the Dakota were indeed unique to their age.

In July of 1864, 40 prisoners from Davenport joined their families at Crow Creek. Their release had been brought about by Dr. Thomas Williamson's unceasing efforts to obtain freedom for the prisoners against whom there were no charges. In April 1864, one year before President Lincoln's assassination, Dr. Williamson visited Washington, D.C., on behalf of the prisoners at Davenport. In a letter from there he exclaimed that his hardest fight was with the Minnesota politicians. The death of Lincoln brought sadness to many of the Dakota, for they realized that their sad cause had lost a sympathetic friend. Had it not been for Lincoln, 400 would have been hanged at Mankato instead of 38.

In June 1866 the Dakota at Crow Creek joined their husbands, fathers, and sons who had finally been released from Camp McClellan near the mouth of the Niobrara River in northeastern Nebraska Territory. After being moved a few miles here and a few miles there, the Santee Reservation eventually was permanently established. The exiles from Minnesota came to be known not as the Mdewakantonwan and Wahpekute Dakota, who were in the majority there, but as the Santee Sioux.

John Williamson and his bride returned to Niobrara on June 10, 1866, at about the same time as the families arrived from Crow Creek. John's brief honeymoon trip had been to the General Assembly of the Presbyterian Church at St. Louis. In July the Prison Church and the Crow Creek Church united to form a church on the Niobrara of over 400 members. In memory of all the tragic pilgrimages of the members, beginning with the sale of their land and their removal to reservations on the Minnesota River, the name of the new church was Pilgrim Church. The next year a prisoner who had converted to Christianity in the prison at Mankato and had become a keen student and eloquent preacher of the Christian gospel at Davenport was elected by the native congregation (both males and females voted!) to be the pastor of the new church. The Reverend Artemas

193

Ehnamani was also proudly reported to be the best deer hunter in the Dakota nation.

But the very first Dakota man to be ordained as a Presbyterian minister was Jean Baptiste Renville, youngest son of the fur trader Joseph Renville—his *Koda Mitawa!* Jean Baptiste's ordination came in the autumn of 1865, but it was the occasion of his being licensed to preach in the spring of that year that led to a revealing incident. Dr. Thomas Williamson preached the sermon at Mankato that opened the meeting of the Dakota Presbytery at which Jean Baptiste Renville was licensed to preach. In his sermon he repeated his plea that had become a refrain—namely, that a great Christian nation should deal justly with the Africans and Indians. That evening a half-breed Dakota who was thought to be one of a party of Hostiles who had come down from Canada and had murdered a pioneer family near Mankato was brought into town and lynched. The incited and excited citizens decided that the murders and the presence in town of that well-known Indian lover Williamson were not just a coincidence. They sent a committee of important Mankato citizens to demand that Dr. Williamson leave town immediately. As one might expect of that gentle man, he quietly left and bore no grudge against the Mankato citizens then or thereafter.

In 1868 the Reverend Jean Baptiste Renville became the pastor of a native church at his old home, Lac qui Parle, and his ruling elder was none other than John Williamson's old friend, Napesni.

Approximately 200 Dakota internees held at Fort Snelling the winter of 1862-63 were not taken to Crow Creek. These were the Friendlies, the majority of them Upper Reservation Dakota who had not taken part in the uprising. Indeed, many had helped white people escape to safety. Regardless of all the evidence proving their help and support to the whites, the whites in Minnesota could not tolerate their presence in the state. General Sibley had them transferred to the eastern part of Dakota Territory near Big Stone Lake, where many of the Wahpetonwans and Sissetons had fled after the defeat of the Lower Reservation Indians. Several of the men served as scouts

194

with the U.S. troops patrolling the border and protecting the white settlers from hostile Indians. Nine Renville names were listed among the scouts. Since a large number of the transferred and refugee Dakota were Christians, Missionary Stephen Riggs helped organize a church called Scouts Camp Church. One of the scouts licensed to preach the gospel to this congregation was Simon Aniwegamani, the first full-blooded Dakota male to profess faith in Jesus Christ. In time two grandsons of Joseph Renville, Daniel and Isaac, were ordained as Presbyterian ministers.

In a report of the Dakota Presbytery in 1882 seven native pastors were listed as serving seven native churches with a total enrollment of 800 members. From 1867 to the end of their lives the two veteran missionaries, Thomas Williamson and Stephen Riggs, spent their summers traveling, supervising, and encouraging the native pastors in their work. Their winters were spent in revising and perfecting their earlier translations of the Bible, begun in the Lac qui Parle days with the help of Joseph Renville and the Pond brothers. The work of a lifetime, the complete Bible in the Dakota language, was completed in 1878-79. Dr. Williamson died June 24, 1879.

After her brother's death, Aunt Jane moved to Greenwood, Dakota Territory, to live with her nephew, John Williamson, who had moved to the Yankton Agency in 1869. Until her death in 1895 Aunt Jane was the beloved great-hearted aunt not only of John's brood of children but also of all the Dakota men, women, and children with whom she spent 52 years of her life.

Alfred Riggs, a lifelong friend of John Williamson and another son of a missionary, took over the work with the Santees on the Niobrara. Under his leadership and with the close guidance of John Williamson and their two fathers, the Santee Normal Training School became the primary educational institution for the Dakota. It is not to be wondered at that the Santee Dakota were the most literate of the Dakota tribes in the northwest in the last quarter of the 19th century.

On behalf of some of the families of Sibley's scouts and other Dakota who had helped the whites and perhaps feared for

their lives among Dakotas who resented that help, Taopi went
to Bishop Whipple, who in turn went to General Sibley and
Alexander Faribault. Knowing that no public or government
support was forthcoming, the three men arranged to settle these
doubly despised Dakota on the private properties of General
Sibley at Mendota and of Alexander Faribault at Faribault.
About 75 tented in Faribault's woodlot and supported themselves by working in his mill, cutting wood, and digging gin-
seng. Obviously their benefactors had to contribute from their
personal funds to help the impoverished Dakota. In 1866 a
gentleman by the name of Ralph Waldo Emerson, on a lecture
tour in Minnesota, visited the Indian camp in Alexander Faribault's woods and wrote of it to his daughter Mary.

Taopi, former chieftain of the farmer Indians, died February
19, 1869. At his bedside in his last hours was his friend, Bishop
Henry Whipple.

Taopi's mother, She Gathers Huckleberries, outlived her son
by four years. She drifted back to the scenes of her childhood
and became a well-known figure on the streets of St. Paul,
where she made a living selling photographs of herself, moccasins, and fur skins. She came to be known as Old Bets. A painting of Old Bets by a local artist hangs in the J. J. Hill Library
in St. Paul. Characteristically, Old Bets resisted Christian Baptism until her end was near. She was baptized on Easter Day
and died a week later in 1873. The citizens of St. Paul raised a
fund to give her what they considered a proper burial at Mendota, although She Gathers Huckleberries would no doubt have
preferred to have been laid on a scaffold on the hills overlooking
Mendota.

Little Crow, the complex chieftain of Kaposia, the reluctant
leader of the uprising, escaped with the remnant of his followers to Canada. The summer after the uprising he returned to
Minnesota, reportedly to steal horses, and was shot and killed
near Hutchinson, Minnesota, while picking black raspberries
with his son. His son was taken to the Santee Normal Training
School, where his name was changed to Thomas Wakeman to
protect him from the animosity to any kin of Little Crow.

Thomas Wakeman eventually became the founder of the Young Men's Christian Association of America among the Dakota people. Little Crow's grandson, Joel Wakeman, was ordained as a pastor and served the native Yellow Medicine Church near Granite Falls.

As for Snana, her name stands on a 50-foot high monument at Birch Coulee to "The Faithful Indians." Folwell writes in *A History of Minnesota* that it was decided to put on the monument "only the names of those full-bloods who had remained unbrokenly loyal and who had saved the life of at least one white person." After a careful consideration of many names, only six stood the test. Snana's is one of them. Remember that Snana was one of the many Dakota children who lived for a time in the Williamson home and absorbed in every pore of their beings the loveliness and lovingness of that home.

The other five names? Other Day, of course. Little Paul, Lorenzo Laurence, Simon Aniwegamani, and Mary Crooks.

To the father and son teams, the Williamsons and the Riggs, there is no monument in stone. There is, however, a trinity of monuments that honors them far more persuasively and powerfully than stone. Two of these they had the joy of seeing with their own eyes—the Dakota Bible and the Dakota Hymn Book. The third is the unique result of their unique efforts—the Dakota Presbytery. It exists today as a nongeographic native enclave within the white Presbyterian church. The 22 organized congregations have an adult membership of 1240 and a constituency of over 4000. Four Dakota pastors, one Chinese-American pastor, and two white pastors serve these native churches.

As for Burning Arrow—One Loon—Kaduza, is there a monument to him anywhere? There is no historical monument to him, nor does the dust of his bones lie in the Earth, his Mother. But his spirit lives in many native Americans today as it once lived in many Dakota. It lives on in many native Americans who are wrestling today with the conflicts with which Kaduza wrestled. This book, then, is in no way a monument for Kaduza, for he still lives on. In the beautiful Dakota tradition of gift-giving, it is simply a gift. A gift to:

Every native American who
    respects the ancient ways,
    respects his blood-relatives,
    respects his *hunka*-relatives,
    respects his relatives the four-leggeds,
    respects his winged relatives,
    respects his little relatives in the grasses,
    respects the waters and the hills,
    respects the whole face of our Mother the Earth;

Every native American who
    worships God, be he called Grandfather or Father of us all,
    worships the Son as the Sun Dancer of the world,
    worships the Holy Spirit sent to our human spirits;

Every native American
    who sees the cross as the Sacred Sun Dance Tree
    where the Son of God danced to his death
    that we might live,
    who sees the risen Christ as the Suffering Servant
    who stands with those who suffer
    to bring their suffering to an end—
    the way of the *heyoka!*

Every native American
    who is ready and willing to forgive the white people
    for causing the uprising and the exile,
    Crow Creek and Wounded Knee,
    because they failed to see what it means
    to be a Christian and a Christ-follower,
    because they failed to see
    that the Christian way
    is contrary to the way of the world.
    It is the way of the *heyoka.*

Mitakuya Owasin!

Glossary

Dakota Names for the Months

January—Moon of Popping Trees

February—Raccoon Moon

March—Moon of Snow Blindness or Sore Eyes

April—Moon of Grass-greening or Snow-melting

May—Planting Moon

June—Moon When the Strawberries Are Red

July—Moon of Chokecherries

August—Moon When the Corn Ripens

September—Moon When Wild Rice Is Harvested

October—Moon When Wild Rice Is Dried

November—Moon When the Deer Rut

December—Moon When the Deer Shed Their Horns

A Glossary of Dakota Words

Akicita (ah-kee′-chee-tah) watchman, police, soldier

Ate (ah-tay′) father

Dakota (dah-ko'-tah) original name of the seven allied tribes now commonly called the Sioux

Hahatonwan (ha-ha-toon'-wahn) Ojibway or Chippewa tribe

Hunka (hoon-kah') relative by choice, selected dear one, an endearing adopted one

Mayawakan (ma-ya-wa'-kan) river flowing into the Minnesota below La qui Parle now called the Chippewa River. Literally, Sacred Cliffs.

Mdewakantons (mm-de-wah'-kan-toon) Spirit Lake people, People of the Mystic Lake, the Dakota band that had its villages on the Mississippi and the Minnesota near the convergence of these two rivers.

Micinksi (mee-cheen'-k-shee) my son

Micunksi (mee-choon'-k-shee) my daughter

Mihigna (mee-heeg'-nah) my husband

Mitakuya Owasin (mee-tah'-coo-yah oh-wa'-sin) I am a relative to all. All my relatives, meaning I am related to all of creation. Words with which the Dakota end all prayers and ceremonies.

Mitawin (mee-tah'-ween) my wife or my woman

Pejuta (pay-zhoo'-tah) literally, medicine

Pejuta wicasta (pay-zhoo'-tah we-cha'-shtah) a healer, or of the root or roots

Sisitonwans (See-see-toon'-wahn) People of the Swamps, the dwellers near marshes, the Dakota tribe or band that lived on the upper Minnesota. They called themselves the Fish Scalers.

Tunkasida (toon-kah'-shee-dah) grandfather

Uncida (oon-chee'-dah) grandmother

200

Wahpekutes (wah-peh'-koo-teh) People Who Shoot Among the Leaves, Dakota band that roamed the headwaters of the Blue Earth and Cannon Rivers. It could also mean shoot through the leaves or leaf shooters.

Wahpetonwans (wah-peh-toon'-wahn) People of the Leaves, dwellers among the leaves. Dakota band that had its villages on the lower Minnesota River.

Wakan (wah-kahn') spiritual, sacred, holy, incomprehensible, or mysterious

Wakantanka (Wah-kahn'-tahn-kah) the Dakota word for God. The Great Spirit, the Creator of All Things, the Great Mystery

Wakpaminisota (wak-pah-mi'-nee-so-tah) the Dakota word for the Minnesota River, which the French fur traders called the St. Pierre and the early pioneers called the St. Peter's River. Literally, The Clear River Water.

Acknowledgments

My mind told me that to write a historical novel about the four Dakota tribes that lived on the land bounded by the Mississippi on the east and the Minnesota on the west until their exile in the spring of 1863 was a dubious enterprise on my part and perhaps an affront to them, whose history I could only research and never directly share.

My heart, however, drummed another message. "Even though you do not qualify as an Indian by government bureau standards," said my heart, "you perhaps qualify as a 'white Indian' because of your lifelong interest in and concern for Indians, and by your subscribing to many of their deeply rooted values."

Obediently and humbly I have followed my heart and written this book. I do not regret it, for I shall never be the same again—nor do I wish to be.

The research part was the easiest and the most exciting, thanks to the excellent resources and the cooperation of the staff of the Division of Archives and Manuscripts of the Minnesota Historical Society. My gratitude to them must include the custodian, who did not force me to remain until opening time in the autumn cold outside the door where Dr. Rune Engebretsen deposited me at 7:45 on his way from Northfield to Bethel College in St. Paul and picked me up again at 5:00 P.M. Thank you, staff! Thank you, Rune!

My admiration for the collections of the Minnesota Historical Society and their availability to unprofessional but nonetheless devoted scholars such as I quadrupled as I went through the boxes of the Thomas S. Williamson and Family Papers, the Stephen R. Riggs and Family Papers, and the American Board of Commissioners of Foreign Missions Papers. Because of the cooperation of the staff, I was able to carry home, in addition to bulging notebooks, many Xerox copies of letters and papers valuable to the writing of this book.

The MINITEX service of the University of Minnesota Library deserves my gratitude for finding and lending me hard-to-obtain books, including *John P. Williamson, a Brother to the Sioux* by Winifred W. Barton.

The St. Olaf College Library was a good source with its collection of Minnesota Historical Journals, county historical publications, histories of Minnesota, and its books about the Dakota before, during, and after their first encounter with white people. It also was my source for literature by Dakota writers, among them Dr. Charles Eastman.

For a too brief and very intense period the Pierre, South Dakota, public library, unbeknownst to its staff, furnished me books from its excellent library of books by and about Indians. Thank you, Jim and Elise Anderson, for continuing to be gracious to a guest who did nothing but read and take notes.

From his father's library Howard Hong brought me a huge and remarkable volume published in 1911 by the Minnesota Historical Society, *The Aborigines of Minnesota*. Later he surprised me with another heavy volume, *A Dakota-English Dictionary*, which he found listed in an antiquarian catalogue from Leipzig, Germany, and ordered for my project. Later yet, when the actual writing began, he listened to the story, chapter by chapter, and was generous with his assent and wise in his dissent. Thank you, *Mihigna!*

The more I read and the more I learned, the more I felt that the Dakota's story must be told—and not from a white person's point of view. The story had to be told, and there could be no lies—neither black nor white nor red lies—or unintentional errors. I was determined to have both Dakota and white scholars carefully and critically read my novel once the mysterious processes of creation had fused this mass of information into a story.

I am deeply grateful to Pastor Paul Boe for reading my completed story and introducing it and me to Pastor Sidney H. Byrd, a native pastor in the Dakota Presbytery of the United Presbyterian Church, and Dr. Chris Cavender, formerly executive director of the Minnesota Sioux tribe. They were my first Dakota readers and critics, and their criticism and advice was most helpful. Pastor Byrd's continuing and continuously encouraging letters buoyed up my faith in and hope for my book when both faith and hope sagged and failed me.

Larry Martin, formerly Indian program coordinator at St. Olaf College, was helpful—even though he is Ojibway, and in the period of which I wrote the Dakota were bitter enemies of the Ojibway!

Father Martin Brokenleg, professor and counselor in native American studies at Augustana College, read the manuscript scrupulously and helped weed out inauthentic attitudes, philosophies, practices, and dialogue.

203

Father Paul B. Steinmetz, Catholic priest on the Pine Ridge Reservation and recipient of a doctor's degree from the University of Stockholm for his dissertation on Dakota religious practices, has read and approved the book.

The white scholars to whom I am also deeply indebted for reading and correcting errors in this historical novel are Dr. Roy W. Meyer of Mankato State University and Dr. Duane Addison of Augustana College, Sioux Falls, South Dakota. Dr. Meyer has published several scholarly books on the Indians with the University of Nebraska Press, but his excellent *History of the Santee Sioux* was the best "white" source for this book.

May I also thank my numerous grandchildren for listening so patiently to the Dakota stories that pour out of me unasked, especially on long summer evenings in our wilderness cabin.